THE COMPLETE BOOK OF
PAPER
AEROPLANES

David Woodroffe

Constable • London

Constable & Robinson Ltd
55-56 Russell Square
London WC1B 4HP

First published in the UK in 2013 by Constable,
an imprint of Constable & Robinson Ltd

A copy of the British Library Cataloguing in Publication Data is
available from the British Library

ISBN 978-1-47211-251-4

Printed and bound in the EU

10 9 8 7 6 5 4 3 2 1

Contents

Introduction

In this book you will find some great ideas and colourful designs for lots of different kinds of paper aircraft. Some are more difficult to make than others, but if you follow the step-by-step instructions, you will get there in the end. If there are a few frustrating, finger-numbing, folds-that-just-won't-crease moments along the way, then it will only serve to make the end result more satisfying and enjoyable!

Although the finished flyers all look fabulous, the vast majority of them are quite simple to make. This isn't rocket science, after all, but it is aviation and all of the models actually fly. Some of the aircraft are best at stunts, some fly better at speed and some excel in a long, sedate glide. They have all been flown successfully by our paper test pilots – Chief Test Pilot/Designer David Woodroffe and his co-pilot Ray Rich. Their proving ground was in the stairwell outside their office, much to the amusement of everyone else in the building. That, of course, is precisely the point of building paper planes – for amusement, for entertainment . . . because it's fun.

Before you get stuck into the fun of folding and flying, however, take a few minutes to read the Pre-Flight Briefing on pages 8 and 9. Not only does it give you some useful tips on paper plane construction and flying techniques, it also points out the important fact that, if you intend to use the actual pages of this book to make your aircraft, you must start from the back of the book. Otherwise, you will end up destroying the instructions for a design you have not yet built.

Once you have gone through the Pre-Flight Briefing, you are cleared for take-off!

Pre-Flight Briefing

MAKING THE PLANES

You will need a pair of scissors to cut out each plane from a photocopy of the page. If you are using the actual pages of the book to

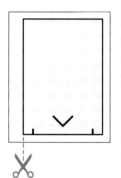

make the planes you should start from the back of the book, otherwise you will lose the left-hand page instructions if you start from the beginning. Cut out along the outer thick line and also cut the lines that will later form tail fins and elevators.

Mountain fold   Valley fold

Folds are made as follows: dashed lines indicate that the paper should be folded away from you (mountain fold), and 'long dash-short dash' lines indicate that the paper should be folded towards you (valley fold). Crease all folds well. Some folds may become quite thick in the later stages of construction, especially when folding the plane in half and folding down the wings, and these will need extra attention.

FLYING THE PLANES

Most of the planes will fly best indoors, either in a large room or corridor. Large stairways where the plane can be launched from the top can make great flying areas. You can fly them outdoors too if conditions are calm but be prepared to lose some over the fence, as it's always the best flyers that escape!

If the plane has a keel hold it there to launch it. If it doesn't have one then hold its rear edge between the thumb and first two fingers.

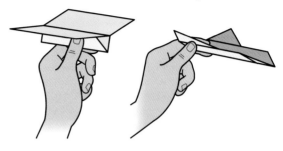

Most planes fly best from a gentle launch so just push the plane away from you and release.

Just like a real plane, a paper plane needs small adjustments to make it fly properly. To achieve an ideal long, straight glide the plane may need to be 'trimmed'. Some of the planes in this book have rear elevators that need to be raised by folding them up, while others will need to have the rear edges of their wings slightly curved up between thumb and finger. Do this if the plane has a tendency to dive.

If the plane banks to the left or the right try raising the rear edge or elevator on the opposite side to the way the plane goes. You can also experiment by bending them down instead of up.

Another way to make sure that the plane flies straight is to check the 'dihedral' of the wings. The 'dihedral angle is formed by the open 'V' shape created when the outer edge of the wing is higher than the inner edge. You will need to hold the plane with its nose pointing towards you and look along its length to see this.

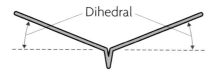
Dihedral

If a draught or gust of wind causes the plane to pitch to one side then the plane will bank in that direction and crash. But if the wings are set with a dihedral then the wing that drops down has a greater area of lift than the side that goes up and so the plane rights itself.

If a plane still refuses to fly evenly check its symmetry. Look along the length of the plane again and see if the front-on shape of one wing is a mirror image of the other. If it isn't, then carefully shape one of the wings between thumb and fingers to match the other.

Some of the planes have tail fins, upturned wing tips or both. These also help the plane to fly straight.

WHY PAPER PLANES FLY

A plane, whether paper or real, needs thrust and lift to fly. Real planes get thrust from engines that push them through the air and then lift is generated by the way that air flows over and under the wing. But paper planes don't have engines, so thrust is firstly applied by the launch and then by gravity. Generally, all paper planes are heavier at the front causing them to dive and go faster, which in turn creates more lift in the wings. Thrust and lift are the forces that make a paper plane fly, whereas gravity and drag are the forces that will eventually bring it back to earth.

FLYING THE KITES

The three kites in this book should be flown in nothing stronger than a light and steady breeze and need to be flown in the correct place. Find a large, flat and uninterrupted area such as a field or a beach, well away from buildings and large hedges which cause turbulence that greatly affects a kite's performance. They should never be flown anywhere near overhead power cables or busy roads, and never near kite-eating trees!

Don't run with a kite: you will be watching the kite and not looking where you are going! If you need to run with a kite then it means that there isn't enough wind to fly it anyway.

SUNSAIL GLIDER

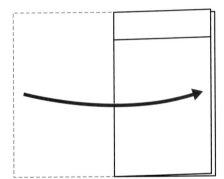

1. With the printed side face down fold down the top edge five times and crease well.

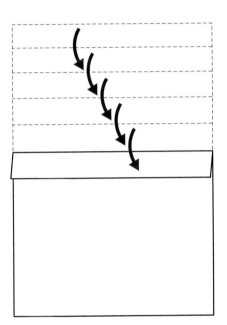

2. Flip over so printed side faces up and fold in half.

3. Open to form a dihedral.

TAKE-OFF TIP

If necessary, curve up the rear edges of the wings between thumb and finger to achieve a smooth glide. Launch gently.

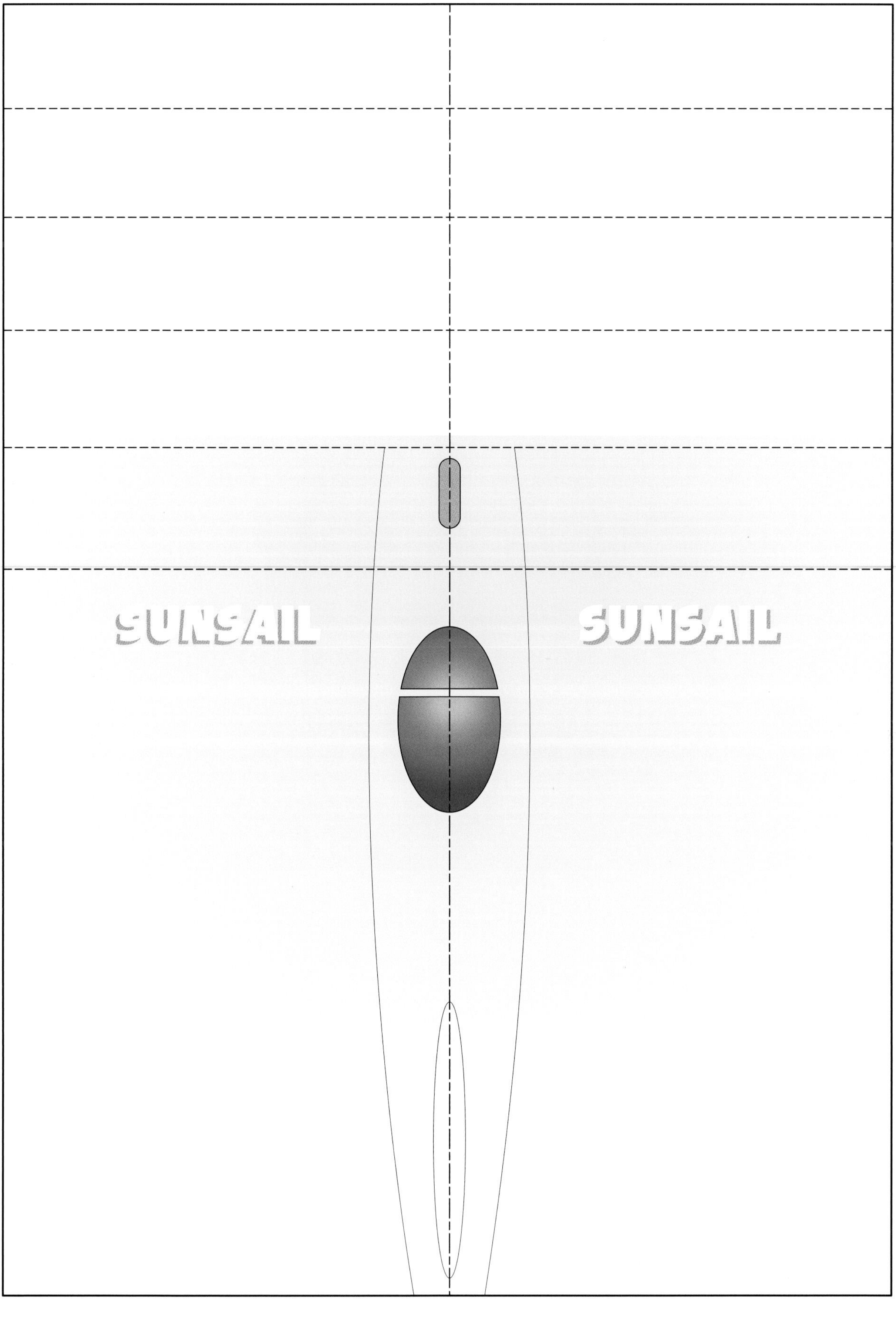
SUNSAIL
SUNSAIL

Stealth Bomber

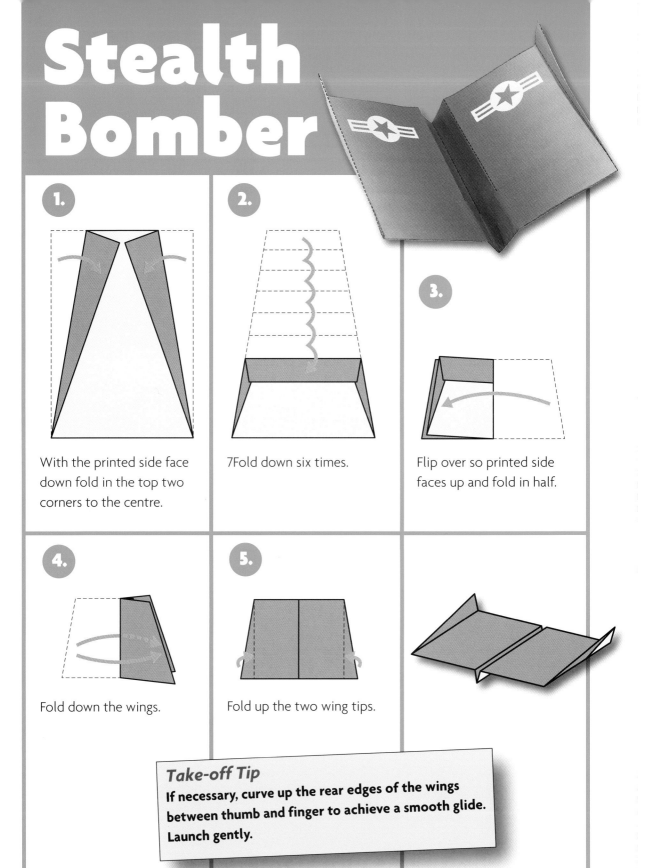

1.

With the printed side face down fold in the top two corners to the centre.

2.

7Fold down six times.

3.

Flip over so printed side faces up and fold in half.

4.

Fold down the wings.

5.

Fold up the two wing tips.

Take-off Tip
If necessary, curve up the rear edges of the wings between thumb and finger to achieve a smooth glide. Launch gently.

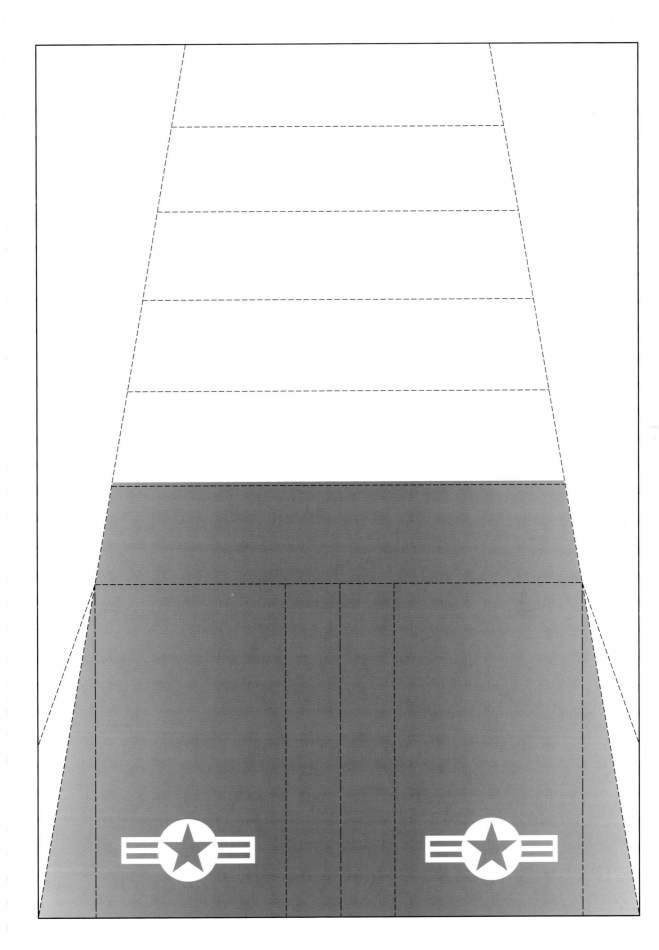

Condor Glider

Take-off Tip
If necessary, curve the rear edges of the wings and tail between thumb and finger to achieve a smooth glide. Launch gently.

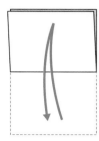

1. With the printed side up fold in half and unfold.

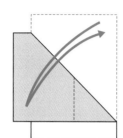

2. Flip over so printed side faces down and fold down the top right corner to bottom left along the mountain fold line and unfold.

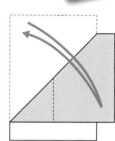

3. Repeat with the left top corner down the the bottom right and unfold.

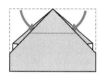

4. Push in the sides along the first fold and collapse to make the top a triangular shape.

5. With the bird's head facing you fold down the top point and crease along the printed mountain fold line, and unfold.

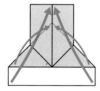

6. Take the bottom left front corner and fold up to shape as shown in the diagram, using the crease formed in step 5. Repeat with the right side.

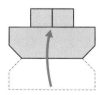

7. Fold up the bottom edge along the fold line.

8. Flip over the plane and fold down the triangular flap.

9. Mountain fold in half.

10. Fold down the wings along the mountain fold lines. Use a small piece of sticky tape across the head to keep the two sides of the body together.

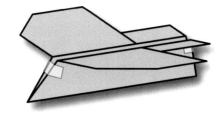

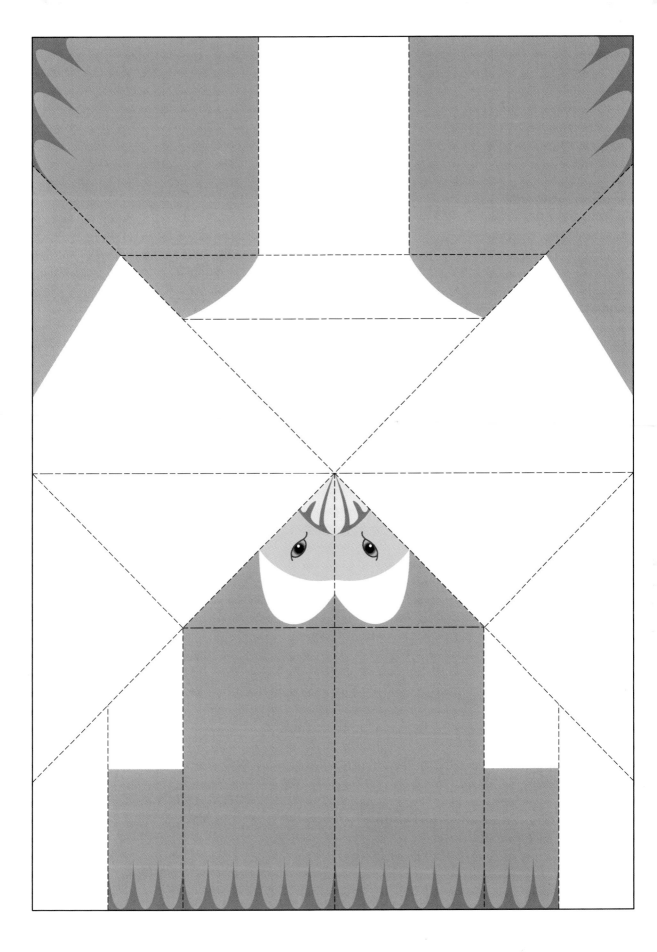

SMILEY SLED KITE

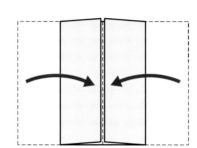

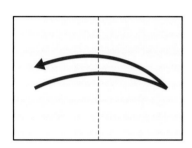

1. With the printed side face up fold in half and unfold.

2. Fold in the two outer edges to the centre.

3. Fold the two edges outwards.

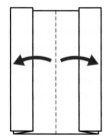

4. Cut 1½ inch (4 cm) strip from a newspaper and tape together to make a tail 4 ft (1.25 m) long.

4 ft (1.25 m)

1½ in (4 cm)

5. Tape the tail to the bottom of the kite. Tie a 3-foot (1 metre) length of button thread through holes made at the dots on each side to make a bridle. Hold the two holes together between finger and thumb of one hand and find the centre point of the bridle and tie a loop. Tie more thread to this loop for a kite line.

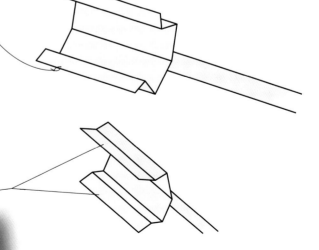

TAKE-OFF TIP
Fly in a gentle wind.

Rapide Missile

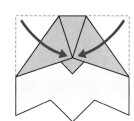

1.

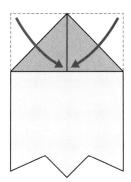

With the printed side face down fold the top two corners down to the centre along the fold lines.

2.

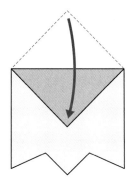

Fold down the top point along the fold line.

3.

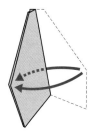

Fold in the top two corners along the fold lines.

4.

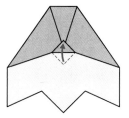

Fold up the tab.

5.

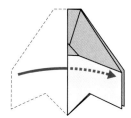

Fold the plane in half.

6.

Fold down the wings.

Take-off Tip
If necessary, curve up the rear edges of the wings between thumb and finger to achieve a smooth glide. Launch gently.

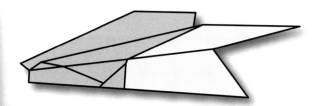

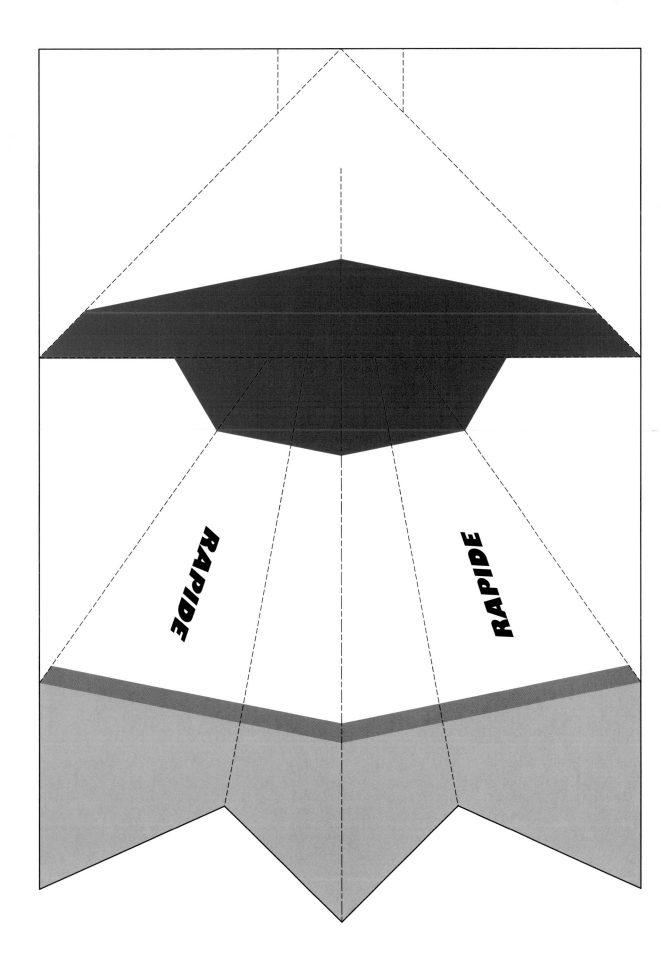

Kestrel Glider

Take-off Tip
If necessary, curve the rear edges of the wings and tail between thumb and finger to achieve a smooth glide. Launch gently.

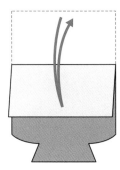

1. With the printed side up fold down the top edge along the valley fold line and unfold.

2. Flip over so printed side faces down and fold down the two top corners along the two angled mountain fold lines.

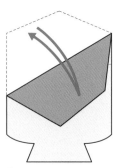

3. Mountain fold the top left edge diagonally and unfold.

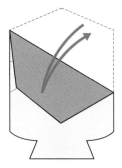

4. Repeat with the top right edge.

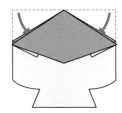

5. Push in the sides along the first fold and collapse to make the top a triangular shape.

6. Crease the short mountain fold between the 'eyes' and then fold down the two top edges.

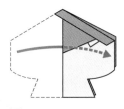

7. Fold in half and crease everything well.

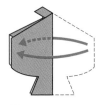

8. Fold down the wings.

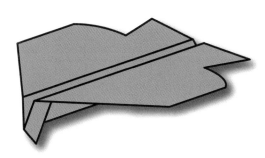

20

CHALLENGER STUNT FLYER

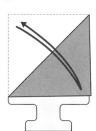

1. With the printed side up fold down the top edge along the valley fold line and unfold.

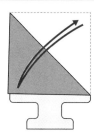

2. Flip over so printed side faces down and fold down the top right corner diagonally along the mountain fold line and unfold.

3. Repeat step two with the left top corner and unfold.

4. Push in the sides along the first fold and collapse to make the top a triangular shape.

5. Take the left loose corner of the triangle and fold diagonally up to the top. Repeat with the right side.

6. Fold up the left corner of the new triangle and crease along the fold line and unfold. Repeat with the right side and unfold.

7. Fold down the left corner of the new triangle and crease along the fold line and unfold. Repeat with the right side and unfold.

8. Crease the small folds between those just created and pinch, press down and crease the folds.

9. Fold back the top tip and crease along the fold line.

10. Fold in half and crease everything well.

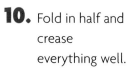

TAKE-OFF TIP
If necessary, curve up the rear edges of the tail between thumb and finger to fly in a loop. Launch forcefully.

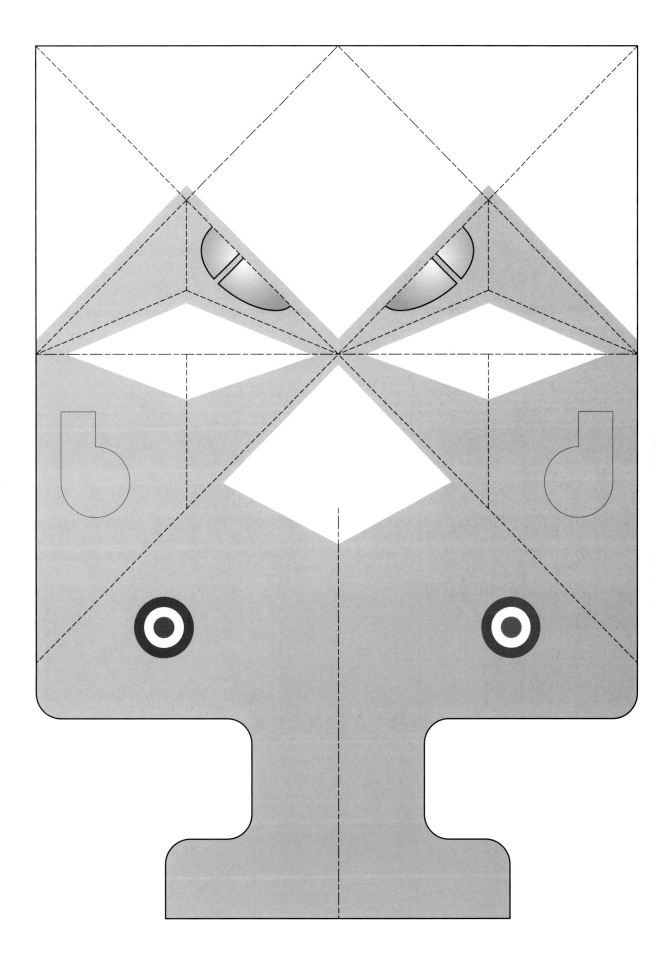

Supersonic Transport

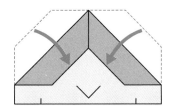

1.

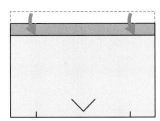

Cut the 'V' shape that will later form the tail fin and the two small cuts for the elevators. With the printed side face down, fold down the long top edge along the mountain fold line.

2.

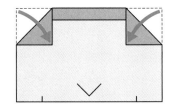

Diagonally fold down the top left corner along the mountain fold line and repeat with the right side.

3.

Fold the new top edges diagonally along the mountain fold lines.

4.

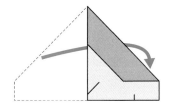

Fold the plane in half.

5.

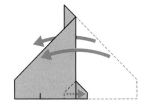

Fold the sides down and push up the tail fin.

6.

Fold up the wings.

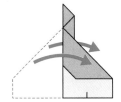

Take-off Tip
Fold up the rear elevators to achieve a smooth glide. Launch gently.

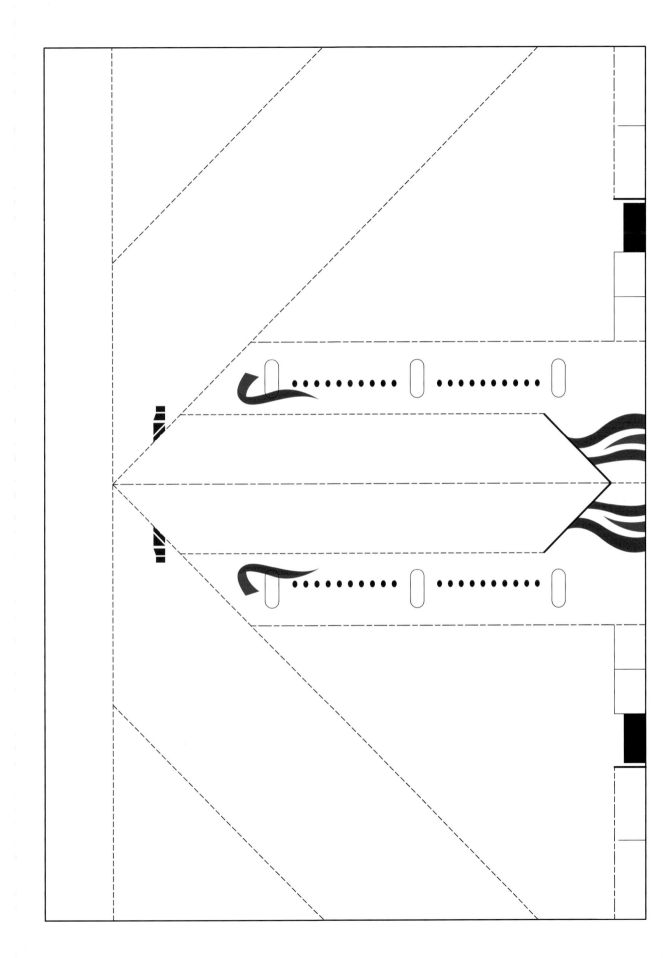

Blue Angel Jet

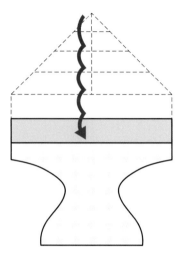

Take-off Tip
If necessary, curve the rear edges of the wings and tail between thumb and finger to achieve a smooth glide. Launch gently.

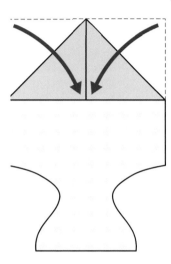

1. With the printed side face down fold in the top two corners to the centre.

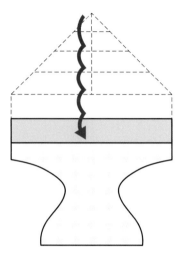

2. Fold down five times.

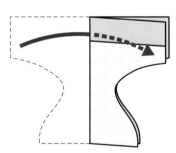

3. Flip over so printed side faces up and fold in half.

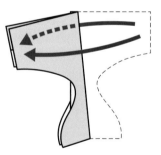

4. Fold down the wings.

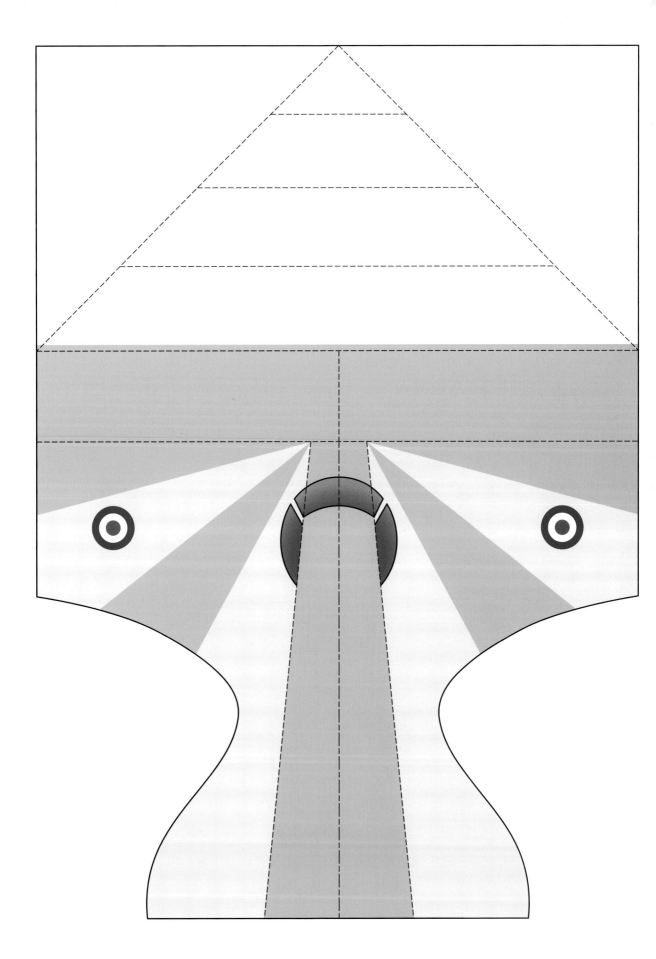

HELLFIRE DIVEBOMBER

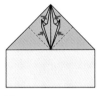

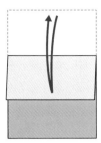

1. With the printed side facing up, fold down the top edge along the valley fold line and unfold.

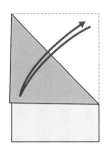

2. Flip over so printed side faces down and fold down the top right corner diagonally along the mountain fold line and unfold.

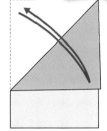

3. Repeat with the left top corner and unfold.

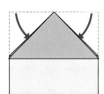

4. Push in the sides along the first fold and collapse to make the top a triangular shape.

5. Take the left loose corner of the triangle and fold diagonally up to the top. Repeat with the right side.

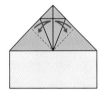

6. Fold up the left corner of the new triangle and crease along the fold line and unfold. Repeat with the right side and unfold.

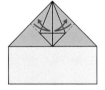

7. Fold down the left corner of the new triangle and crease along the fold line and unfold. Repeat with the right side and unfold.

8. Crease the small folds between those just created and pinch, press down and crease the folds.

9. Fold back the top tip and crease along the fold line.

10. Fold in half and crease everything well.

11. Fold up the wing tips to create the profile shown.

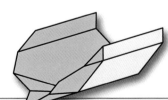

TAKE-OFF TIP

If necessary, curve up the rear edges of the wings between thumb and finger to achieve a smooth glide. Launch gently.

28

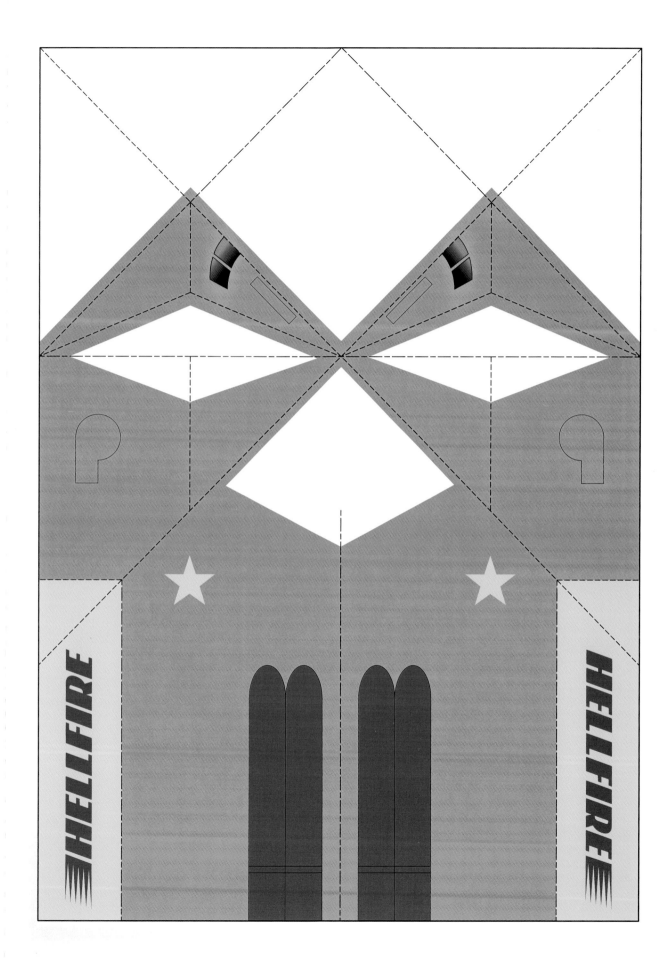

Blackbird Reconnaissance Aircraft

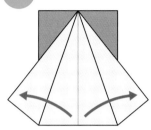

 1.

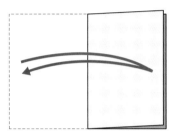

With the printed side face up fold in half and unfold.

2.

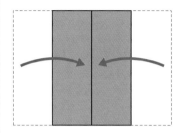

Flip over so printed side faces down and fold in the two outer edges to the centre.

3.

Fold out the bottom corners from the centre along the valley fold lines.

4.

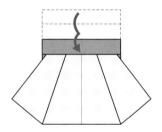

Fold down the top edge twice.

5.

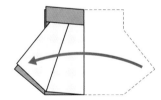

Fold in half.

6.

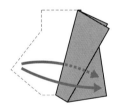

Fold down the wings.

Take-off Tip

If necessary, curve up the rear edges of the wings between thumb and finger to achieve a smooth glide. Launch at moderate speed.

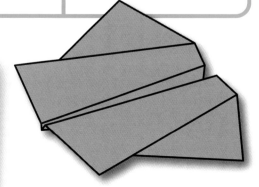

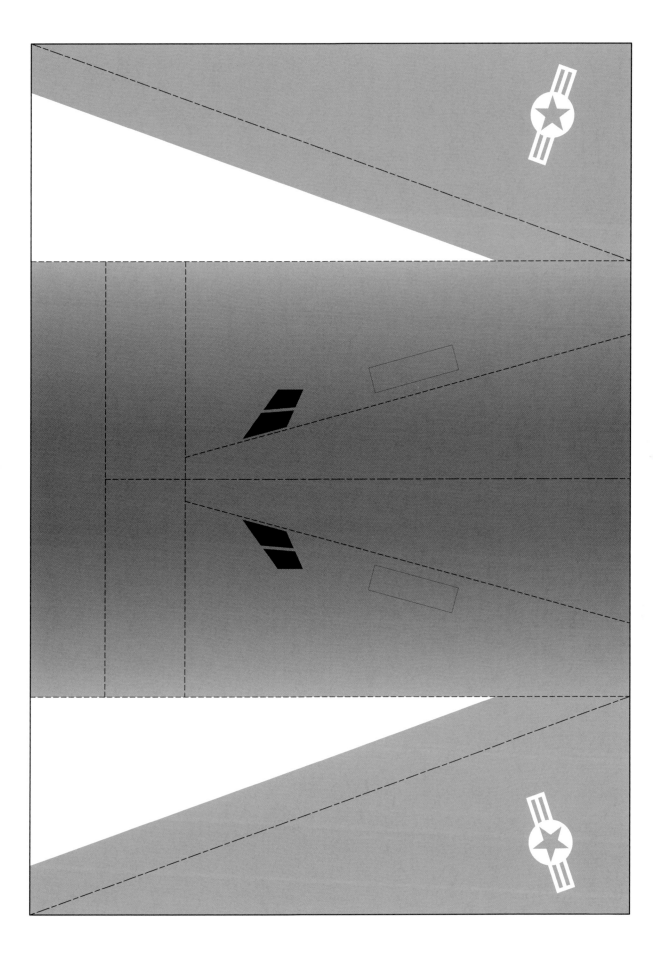

Spitfire Fighter

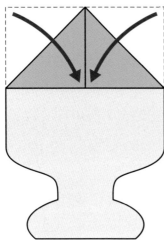

1. With the printed side face down fold in the top two corners to the centre.

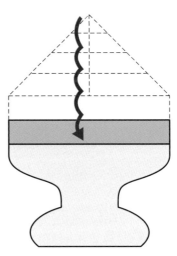

2. Fold down five times.

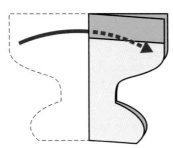

3. Flip over so printed side faces up and fold in half.

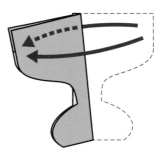

4. Fold down the wings.

Take-off Tip

If necessary, curve up the rear edges of the wings and tail between thumb and finger to achieve a smooth glide. Launch gently.

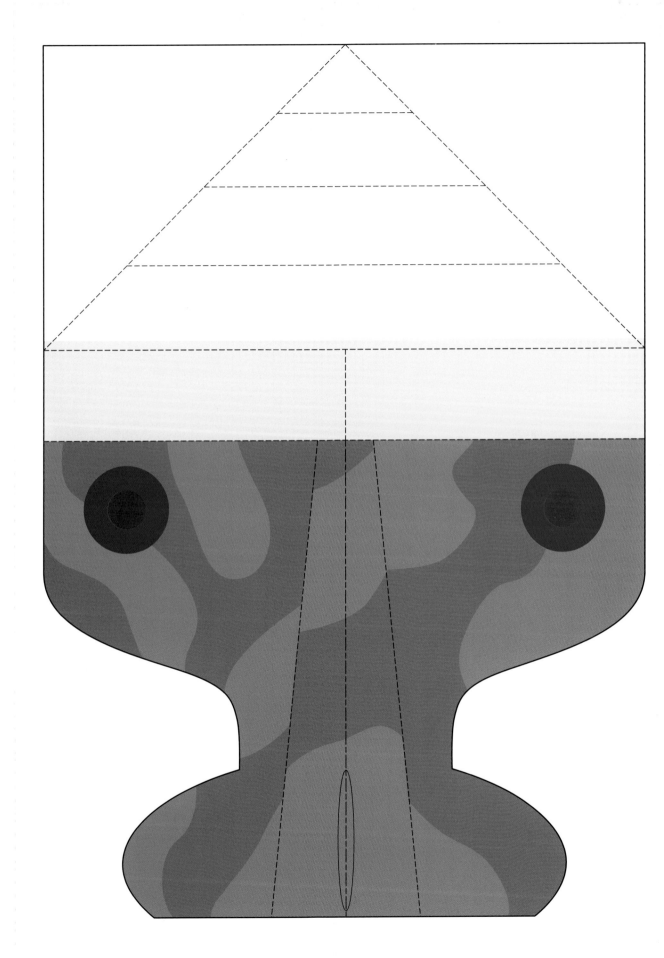

DRAGON KITE

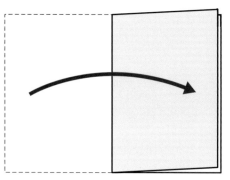

1. Lay the sheet printed side down and fold in half.

2. Fold down the wings.

3. Staple the red keel together.

4. Open the wings and tape a thin piece of bamboo strip, or a kebeb stick (cut the sharp ends off first) to the back of them as shown.

5. Tie button thread through one of towing points, shown as black dots along the keel (start with the centre one first).

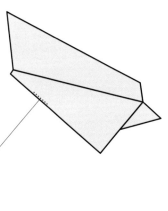

TAKE-OFF TIP

Fly in a gentle breeze and try threading the line through different towing points until the kite flies well. You can even try attaching a tail as in the sled kite.

Stargazer
Spacecraft

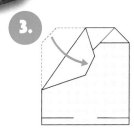

1.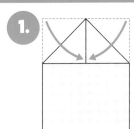

With the printed side face down fold in the top two corners to the centre.

2.

Fold down the top point along the mountain fold line.

3.

Diagonally fold down the top left edge and crease along the mountain fold line.

4.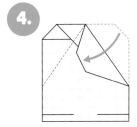

Fold back the flap created in step 3 and repeat with the right side.

5.

Flip the plane over and fold it in half. Then fold down the flaps created in stages 3 and 4.

6.

Fold down the wings.

7.

Curve up the two flaps at the rear of the wings and tape together.

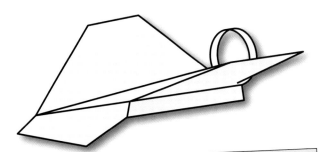

Take-off Tip

If necessary, curve up the rear edges of the wings between thumb and finger to achieve a smooth glide. Launch gently.

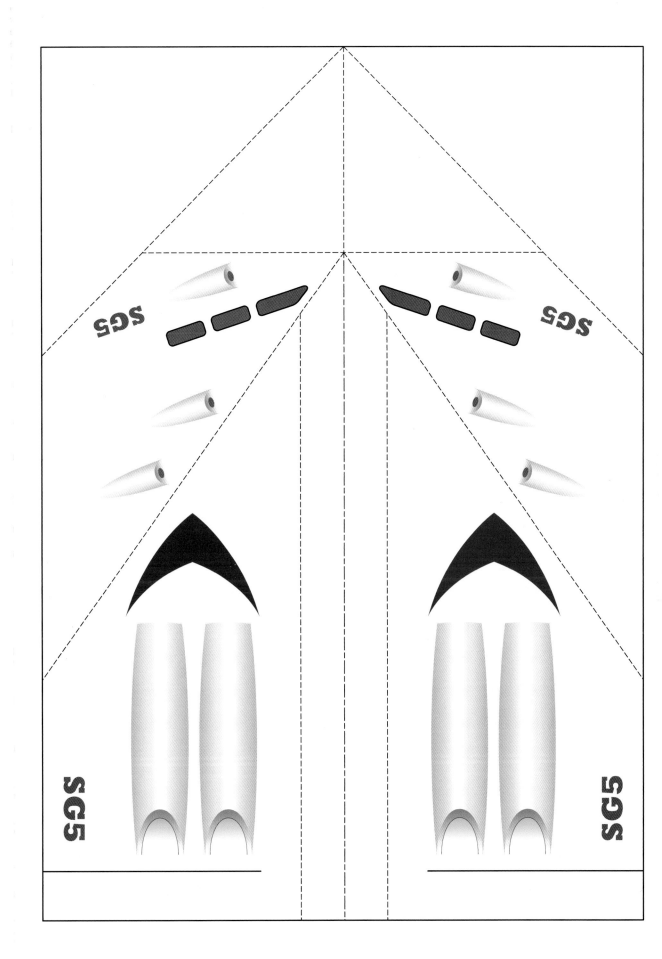

Hornet Fighter

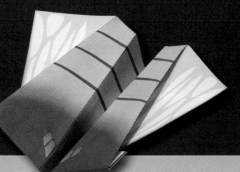

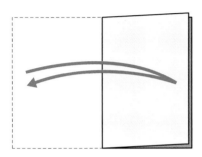

1. With the printed side face up fold in half and unfold.

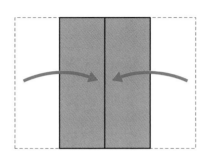

2. Flip over so printed side faces down and fold in the two outer edges to the centre.

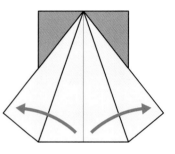

3. Fold out the bottom corners from the centre along the valley fold lines.

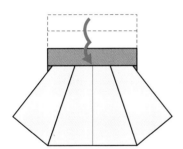

4. Fold down the top edge twice.

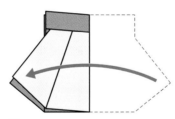

5. Fold in half.

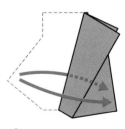

6. Fold down the wings.

Take-off Tip

If necessary, curve up the rear edges of the wings between thumb and finger to achieve a smooth glide. Launch at moderate speed.

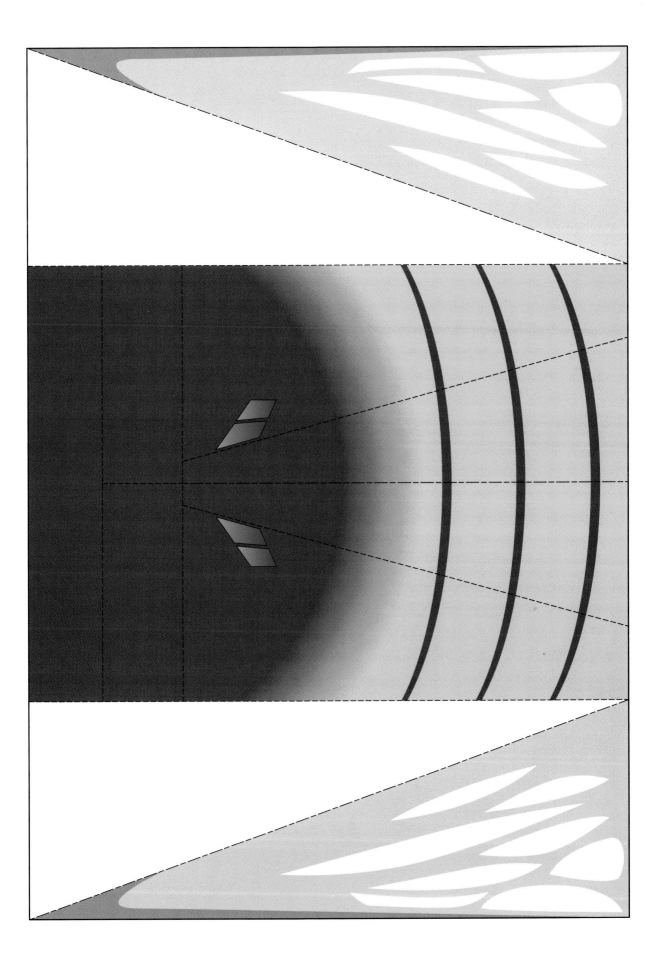

THUNDERCLOUD BOMBER

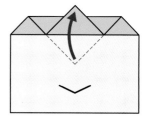

1. Cut the 'V' shape that will later form the tail fin. With the printed side face down, fold down the top edge twice along the mountain fold lines.

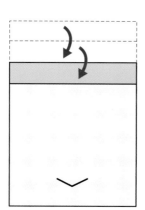

2. Diagonally fold down the top left corner along the mountain fold line and repeat with the right side.

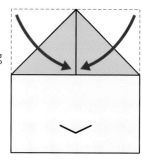

3. Fold down the top point along the mountain fold line.

4. Fold up the point along the fold lines.

5. Fold the plane in half.

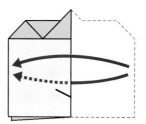

6. Fold the wings down and push up the tail fin.

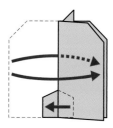

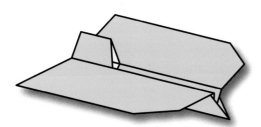

TAKE-OFF TIP
If necessary, curve up the rear edges of the wings between thumb and finger to achieve a smooth glide. Launch gently.

Ghost Stealth Fighter

1.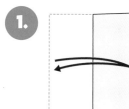

With the printed side face down fold down the left edge across to the right edge, crease and then unfold.

2.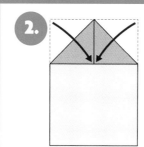

Flip the plane over and diagonally fold down the top left corner along the mountain fold line and repeat with the right side.

3.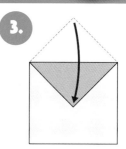

Fold down the top triangle along the mountain fold line.

4.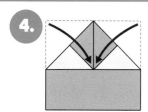

Flip the plane over and diagonally fold down the two top corners.

5.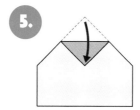

Flip the plane back and fold down the top point.

6.

Flip the plane over again and crease the small diagonal folds and then lift the folds upwards and crease the new shape.

7.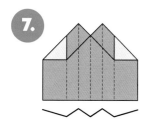

Fold the mountain and valley folds to create the profile shown.

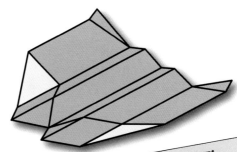

Take-off Tip
Fold up the rear elevators to achieve a smooth glide. Launch gently.

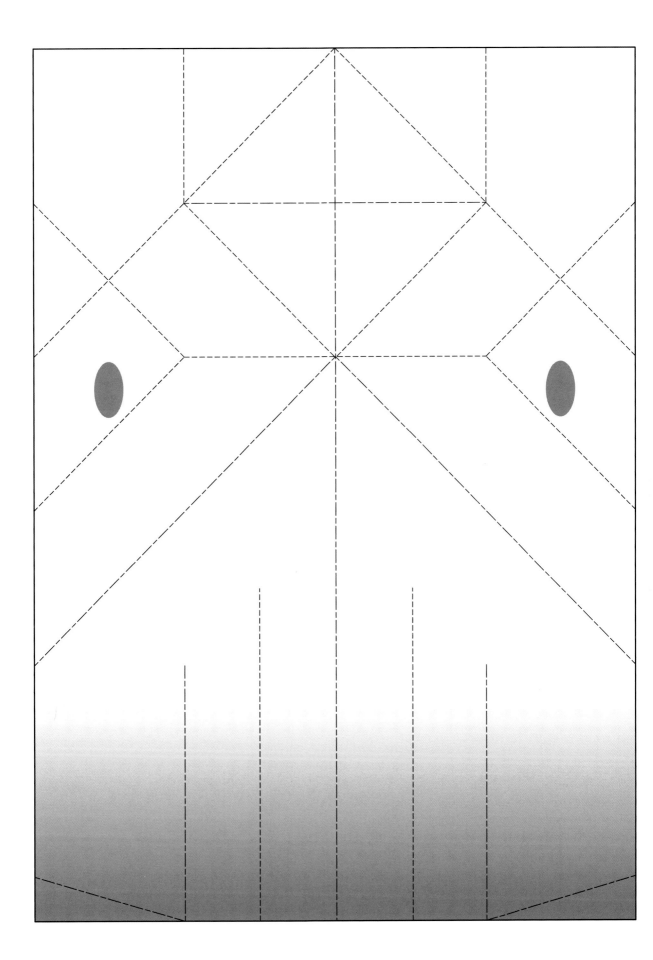

Sky Warrior Bomber

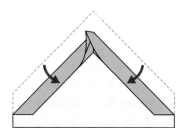

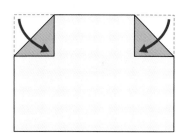

1. With the printed side face down, fold over the top two corners along the mountain fold lines.

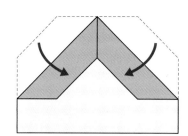

2. Fold down the two new edges along the mountain fold lines.

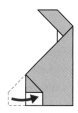

3. Crease the short mountain fold between the 'windows' and then fold down the two top edges.

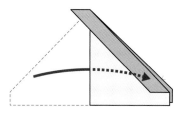

4. Fold in half and crease everything well.

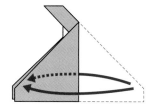

5. Fold down the wings.

6. Fold up the wing tips.

Take-off Tip

Fold up the rear elevators to achieve a smooth glide. Launch gently.

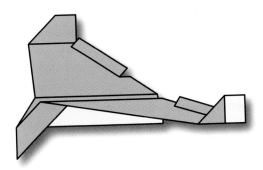

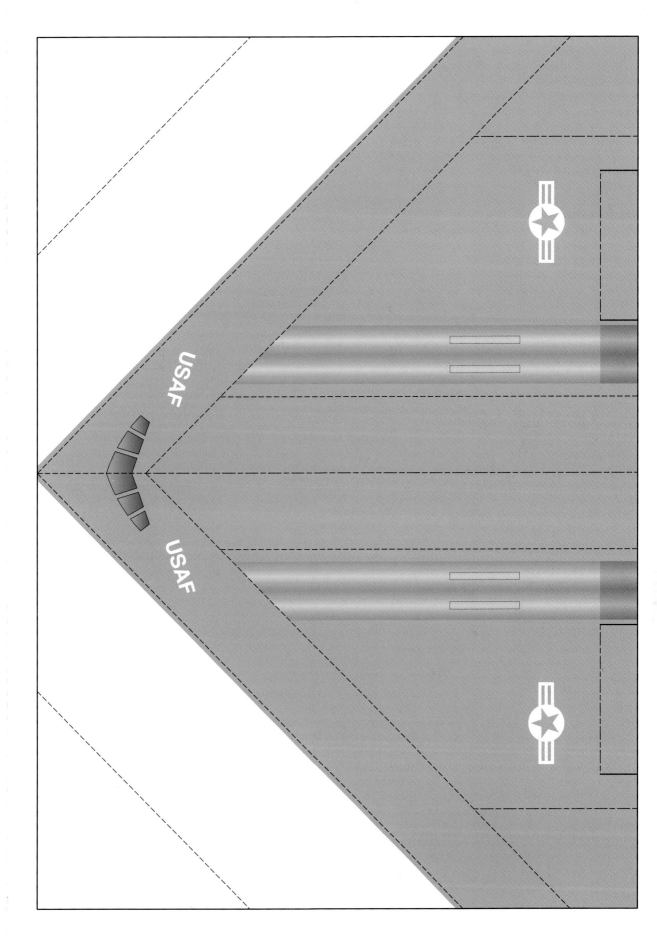

RED ARROW JET

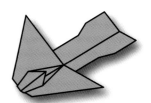

TAKE-OFF TIP

If necessary, curve up the rear edges of the tail between thumb and finger to fly in a loop. **Launch forcefully**.

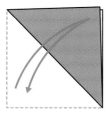

1. Cut out the square that is the main part of the plane and, with the printed side face down, fold the bottom right corner up the top left, crease and then unfold.

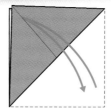

2. Repeat step 1 with the bottom right corner.

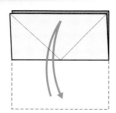

3. Flip over so printed side faces up and fold the bottom edge up to the top edge, crease and then unfold.

4. Fold the left edge over to the right edge, crease and then unfold.

5. Push in the sides along the valley folds and collapse to make a triangular shape.

6. Take the left loose corner of the triangle and fold diagonally up to the top. Repeat with the right side.

7. Fold up the left corner of the new triangle and crease along the fold line and unfold. Repeat with the right side and unfold.

8. Fold down the left corner of the new triangle and crease along the fold line and unfold. Repeat with the right side and unfold.

9. Crease the small folds between those just created and pinch, press down and crease the folds.

10. Fold back the two points created in step 9.

11. Cut out the tail and fold down the two top corners.

12. Push the tail into the plane so the point fits into the nose.

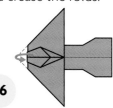

13. Fold the nose over.

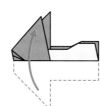

14. Fold the plane in half.

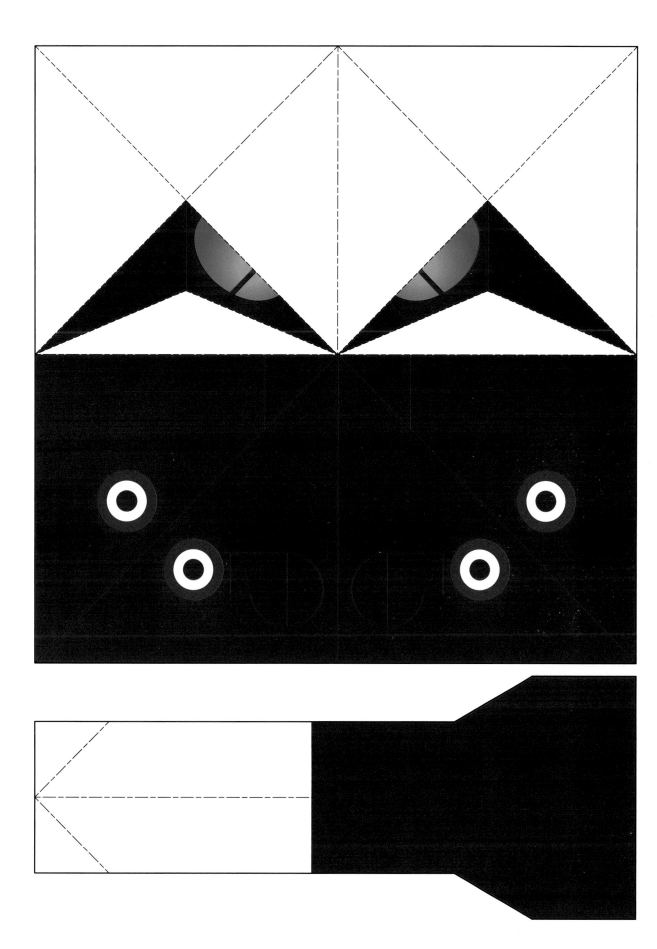

Shadow Space Gunship

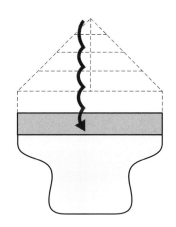

1.

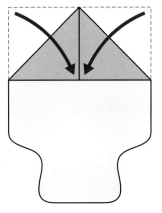

With the printed side face down fold in the top two corners to the centre.

2.

Fold down five times.

3.

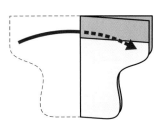

Flip over so printed side faces up and fold in half.

4.

Fold down the wings.

Take-off Tip

If necessary, curve up the rear edges of the wings and tail between thumb and finger to achieve a smooth glide. Launch gently.

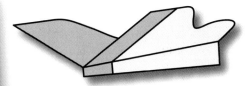

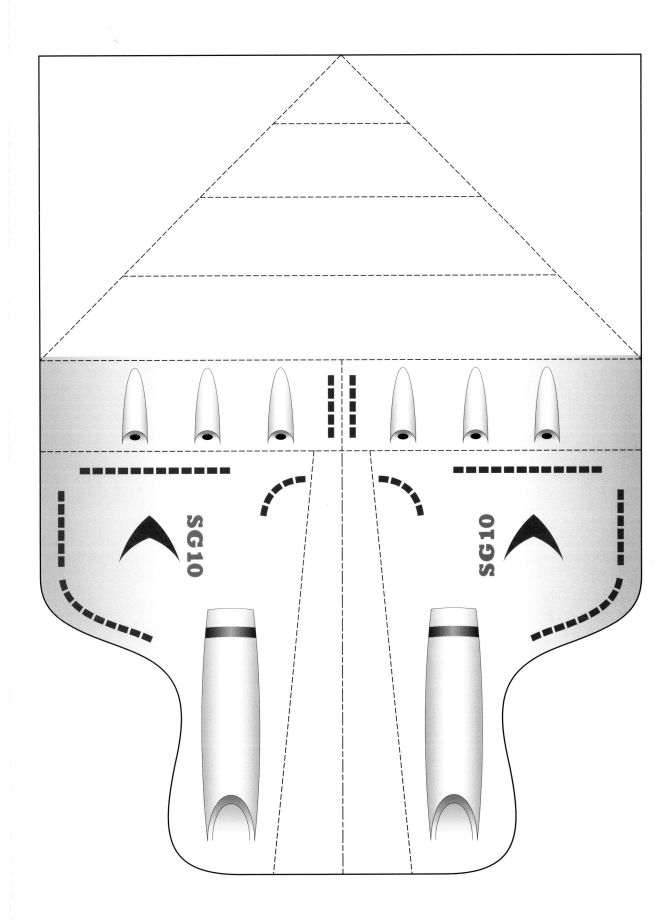

SG10

SG10

Flivver Ground Effect Aircraft

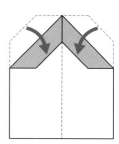

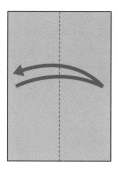

1. With the printed side face up, fold in half and then unfold.

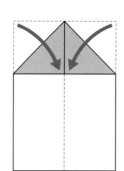

2. Flip over so printed side faces down and diagonally fold in the two top corners to the centre.

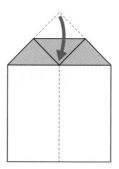

3. Fold down the top tip along the mountain fold line.

4. Fold down the two new top edges along the mountain fold lines.

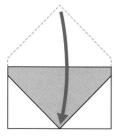

5. Fold down the top tip to line up with the bottom edge.

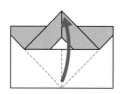

6. Fold up the tip and crease along the mountain fold line.

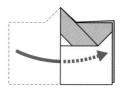

7. Fold the plane in half.

8. Fold down the wings and fold up the wing tips.

Take-off Tip

If necessary, curve up the rear edges of the wings between thumb and finger to achieve a smooth glide. Launch gently.

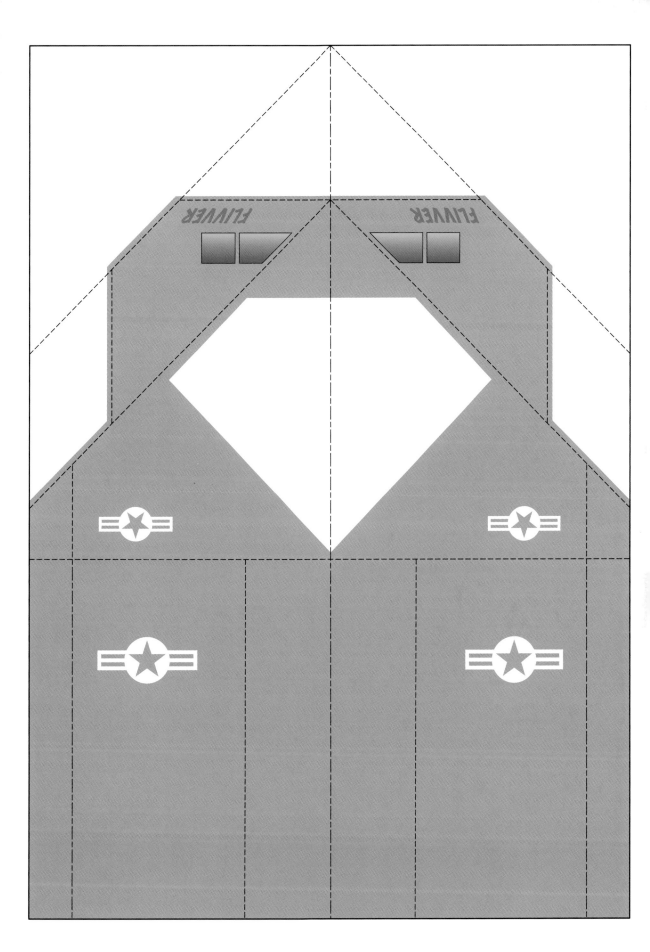

SWOOP GLIDER

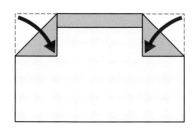

1. With the printed side face down, fold the top edge down along the fold line.

2. Diagonally fold down the top left corner along the mountain fold line and repeat with the right side.

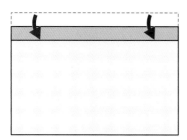

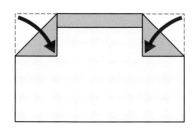

3. Diagonally fold down the two new top edges along the mountain fold lines.

4. Fold the plane in half.

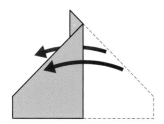

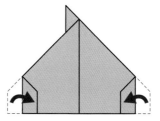

5. Fold down the wings.

6. Fold up the wing tips.

TAKE-OFF TIP
If necessary, curve up the rear edges of the wings between thumb and finger to achieve a smooth glide. Launch gently.

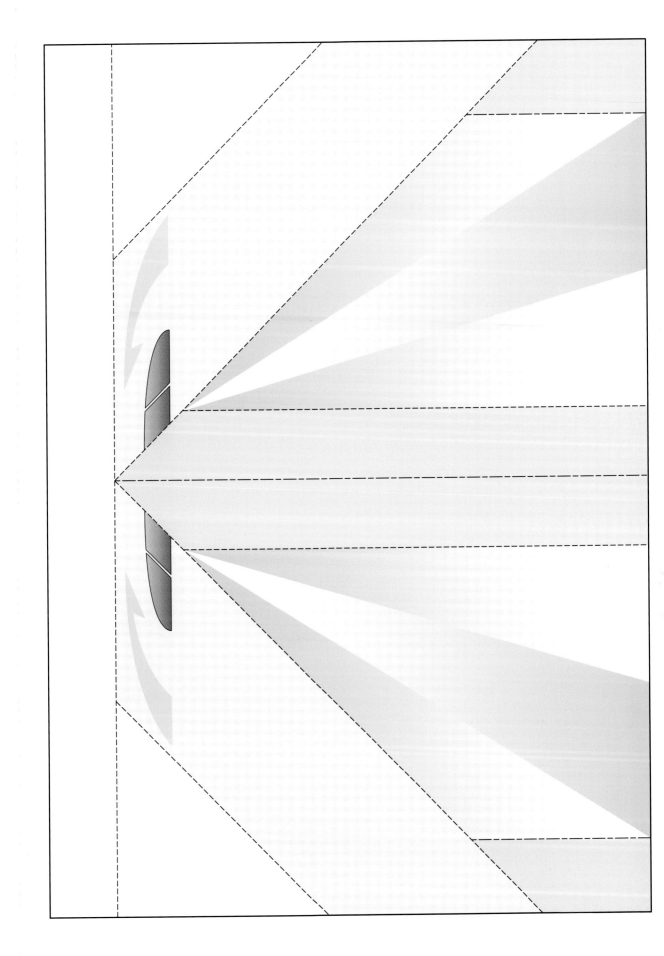

Wedge Fighter

1.

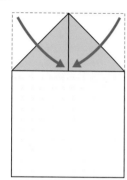

Lay the sheet printed side down and diagonally fold in the two top corners.

2.

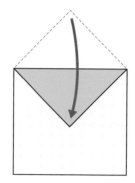

Fold down the top point along the mountain fold line.

3.

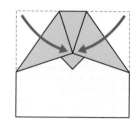

Fold the two new top corners into the centre along the mountain fold lines.

4.

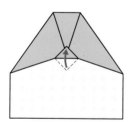

Fold up the small tab.

5.

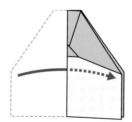

Fold the plane in half.

6.

Fold down the wings.

Take-off Tip
If necessary, curve up the rear edges of the wings between thumb and finger to achieve a smooth glide. Launch at a moderate speed.

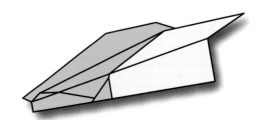

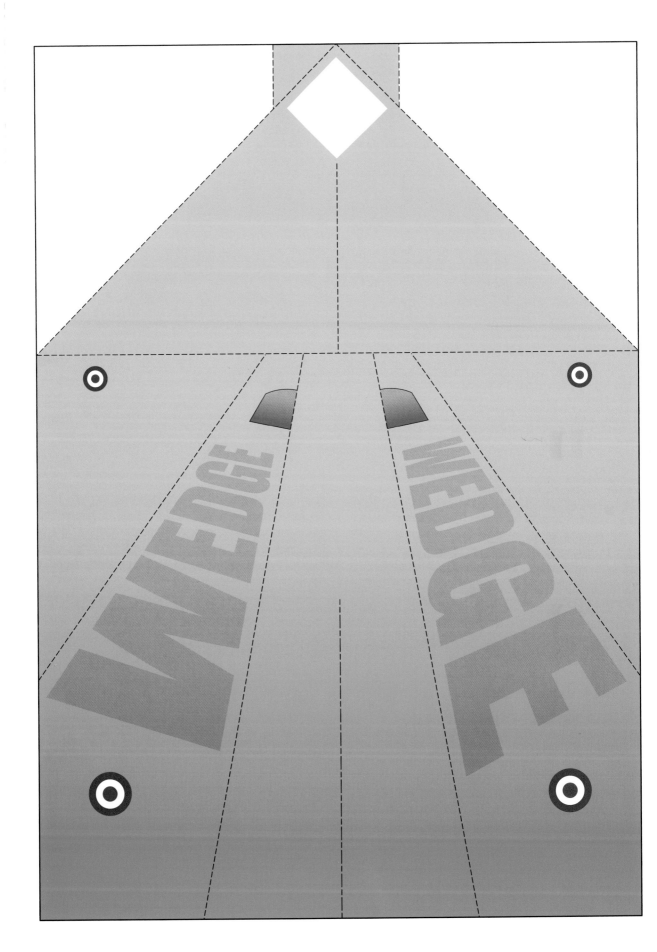

SunBeam Space Transport

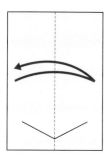

1. Cut the 'V' shape that will later form the raised tail. Lay the sheet printed side up and fold in half and then unfold.

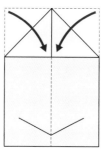

2. Flip over so printed side faces down and fold down the top left corner diagonally along the mountain fold line. Repeat with the right corner.

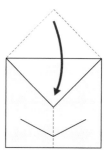

3. Fold down the top tip along the mountain fold line.

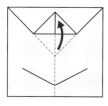

4. Fold up the tip along the mountain fold line.

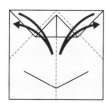

5. Diagonally fold down the 2 top corners to the centre. Crease and then unfold.

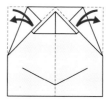

6. Fold the same two top corners to the crease created in step 5 and then unfold.

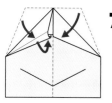

7. Fold up the tip along the mountain fold line. Tuck the flaps created in step 6 under the tip folded in step 4.

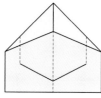

8. Diagonally fold down the two top corners to the centre. Crease and then unfold.

Take-off Tip

If necessary, curve up the rear edges of the wings between thumb and finger to achieve a smooth glide. Launch gently.

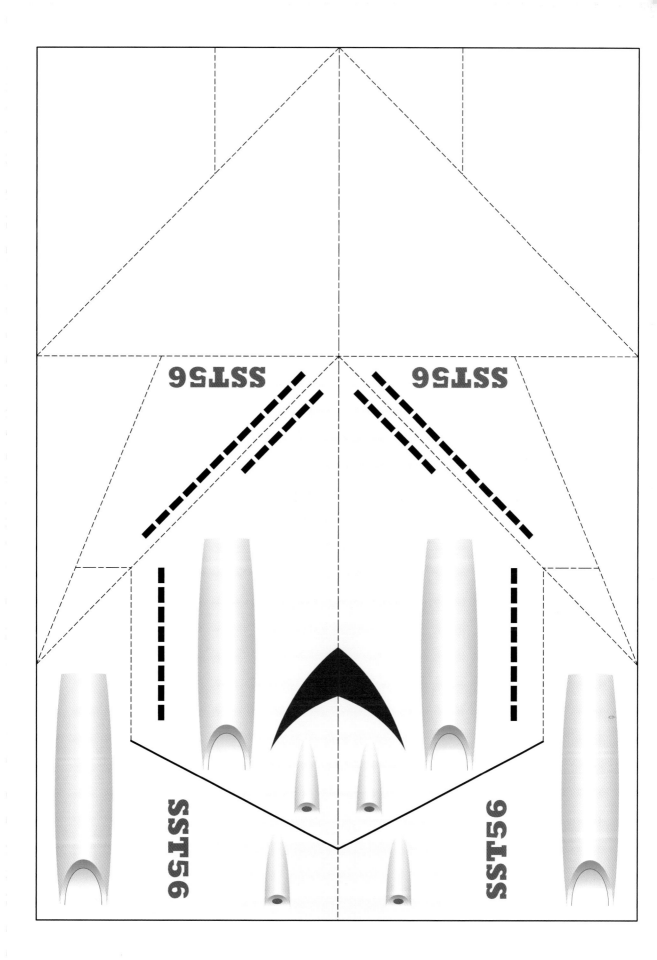

DEMON DIVEBOMBER

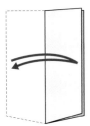

1. With the printed side face up, fold in half and then unfold.

2. Flip over so printed side faces down and fold down the top left corner diagonally along the mountain fold line and unfold. Repeat with the right corner and unfold.

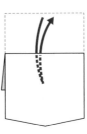

3. Fold back the top edge along the valley fold line and then unfold.

4. Push in the sides along the valley folds and collapse to make a triangular shape.

5. Take the left loose corner of the triangle and fold diagonally up to the top and then unfold. Repeat with the right side.

6. Take the same left loose corner in step 5 and fold inwards to the centre and then unfold. Repeat with the right side.

7. Fold down the top point to line up with the bottom centre of the triangle, crease and the unfold.

8. The plane with it's creased lines should now look like this.

9. Lift the single bottom edge of the triangle, fold it up and crease along the valley fold line. Lift up the two bottom corners of the triangle and position them over the top point.

10. Crease and your plane should now look like this.

11. Diagonally fold out the two top inner points.

12. Fold down the top flap along the mountain fold line.

13. Fold in half.

14. Fold down the wings.

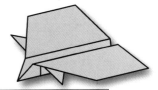

TAKE-OFF TIP If necessary, curve up the rear edges of the wings between thumb and finger to achieve a smooth glide. Launch gently.

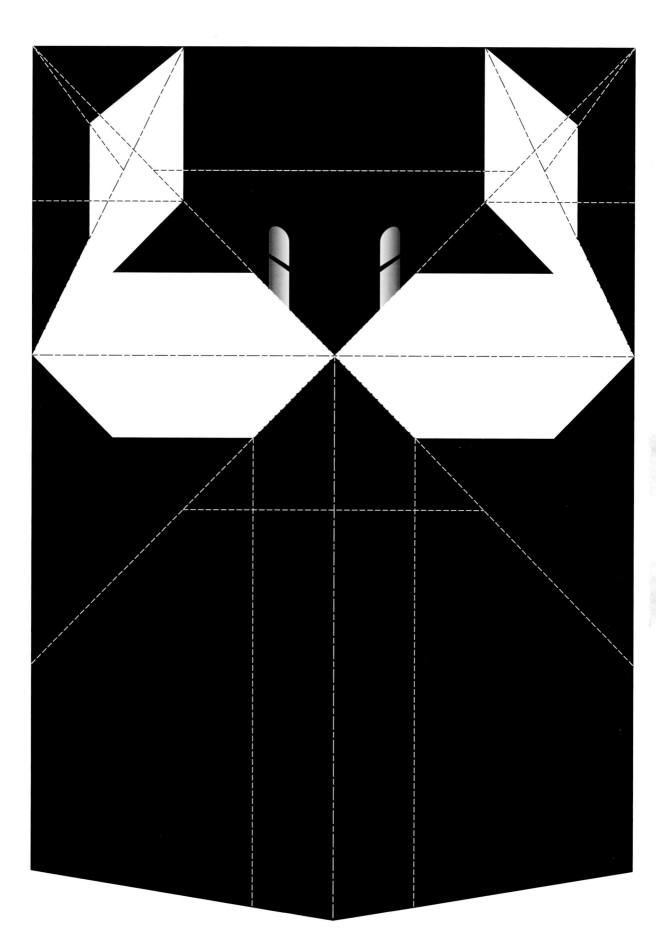

Galactic Transporter

1.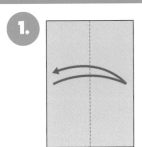

With the printed side facing up, fold in half and then unfold.

2.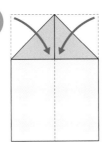

Flip the plane over and fold the top left corner into the central crease. Repeat with the right corner.

3.

Fold the top point downwards.

4.

Fold the point upwards to the printed line.

5.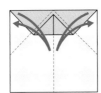

Fold the top left corner into the centre then crease and unfold. Repeat with right corner.

6.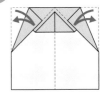

Fold the left edge to the crease created in 5 and then unfold. Repeat with the right edge.

7.

Fold the large right angled triangles created in 5 over again. Tuck the flaps created in 6 under the tip folded in 4.

8.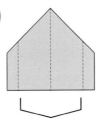

Flip the plane back, fold up the wing tips and create the profile shown.

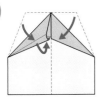

Take-off Tip
Launch gently.

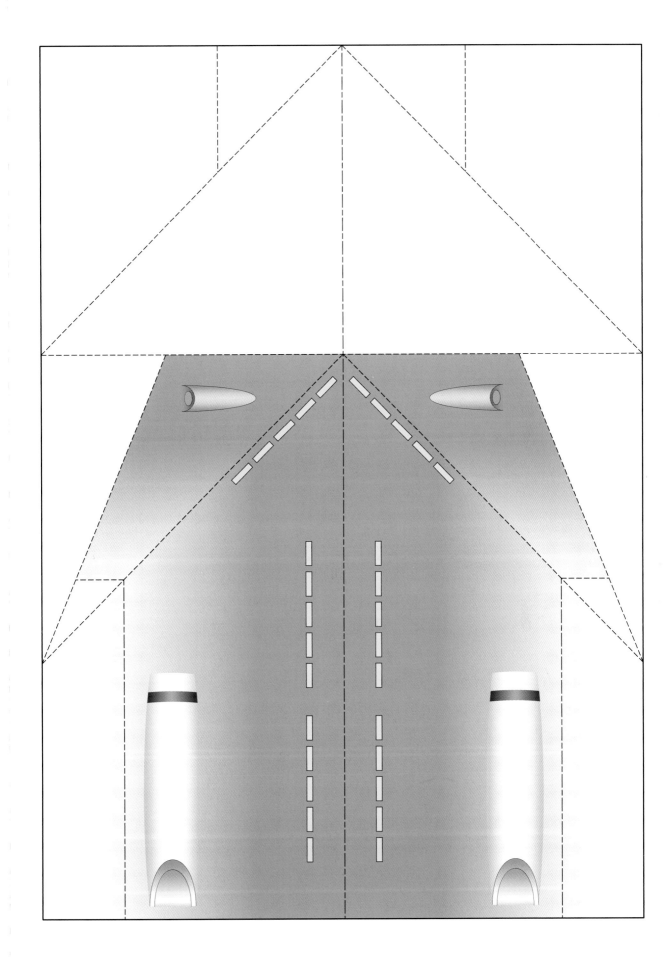

Flaming Sword Interceptor

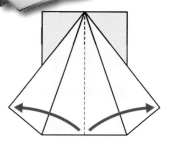

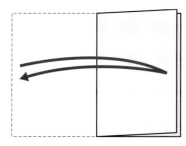

1. With the printed side face up, fold in half and unfold.

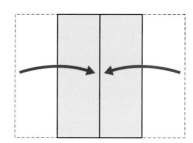

2. Flip over so printed side faces down and fold in the two outer edges to the centre.

3. Fold out the bottom corners from the centre along the valley fold lines.

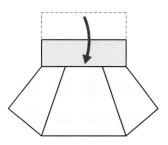

4. Fold down the top edge.

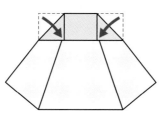

5. Diagonally fold in the two top corners.

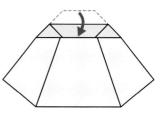

6. Fold down the top edge along the mountain fold line.

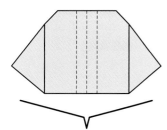

7. Fold in half and fold down the wings. Tape the two front edges of the body together with a small piece of sticky tape.

Take-off Tip

If necessary, curve up the rear edges of the wings between thumb and finger to achieve a smooth glide. Launch gently.

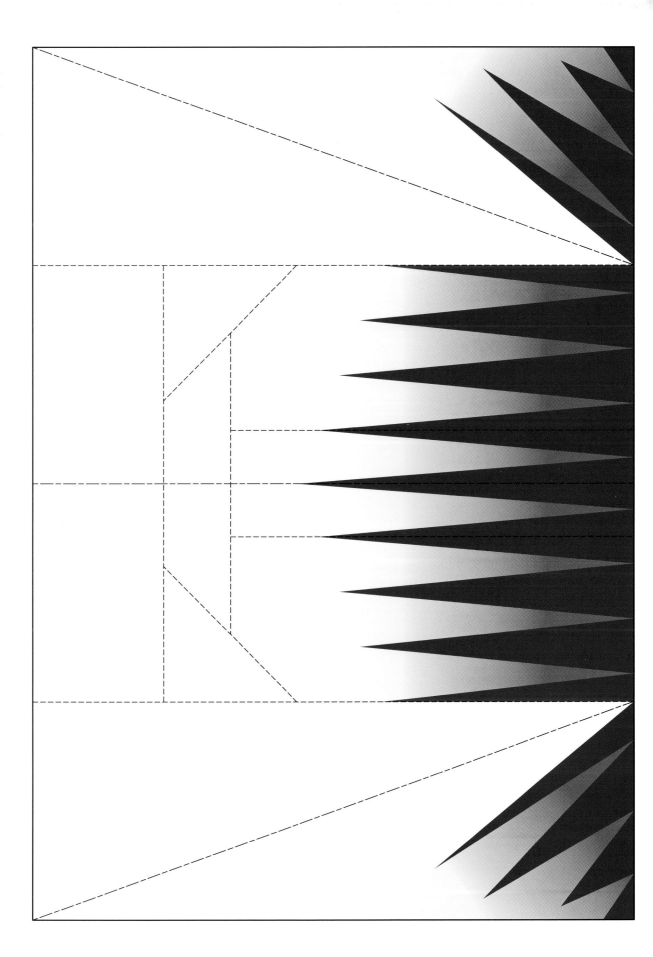

RAVEN NIGHT FIGHTER

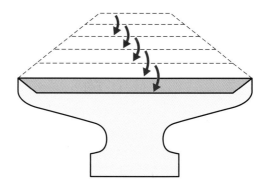

1. Lay the sheet printed side down and fold down the top edge five times.

2. Fold in half, fold down the wings and fold up the wing tips to create the profile shown.

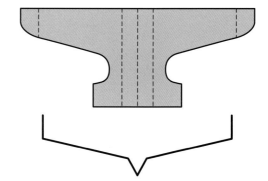

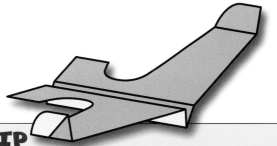

TAKE-OFF TIP
If necessary, curve up the rear edges of the wings and tail between thumb and finger to achieve a smooth glide. Launch gently.

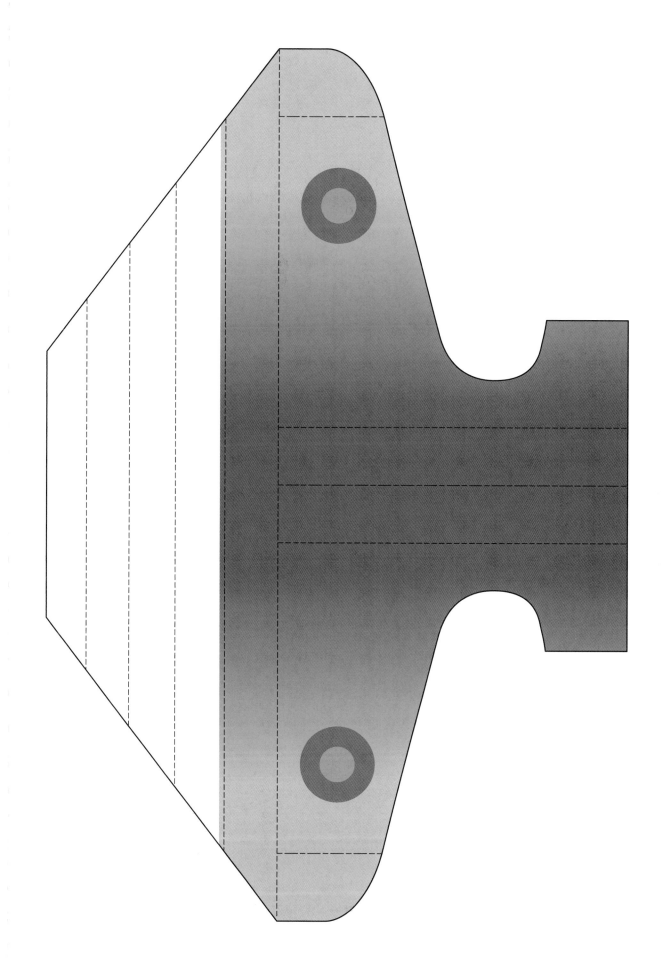

Superfortress Bomber

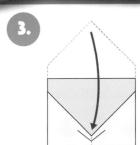

1.

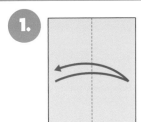

Cut the 'V' shape that will later form the raised tail. With the printed side facing up fold the left edge to the right one, crease and then unfold.

2.

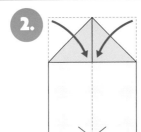

Fold in the two top corners along the mountain fold lines.

3.

Fold down the top point along the mountain fold line.

4.

Fold in the two top corners along the mountain fold lines.

5.

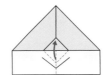

Fold up the small pointed tab along the fold line.

6.

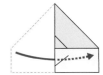

Fold the plane in half.

7.

Fold down the wings and push up the tail fin.

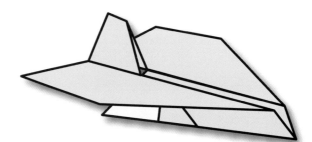

Take-off Tip
If necessary, curve up the rear edges of the wings between thumb and finger to achieve a smooth glide. Launch gently.

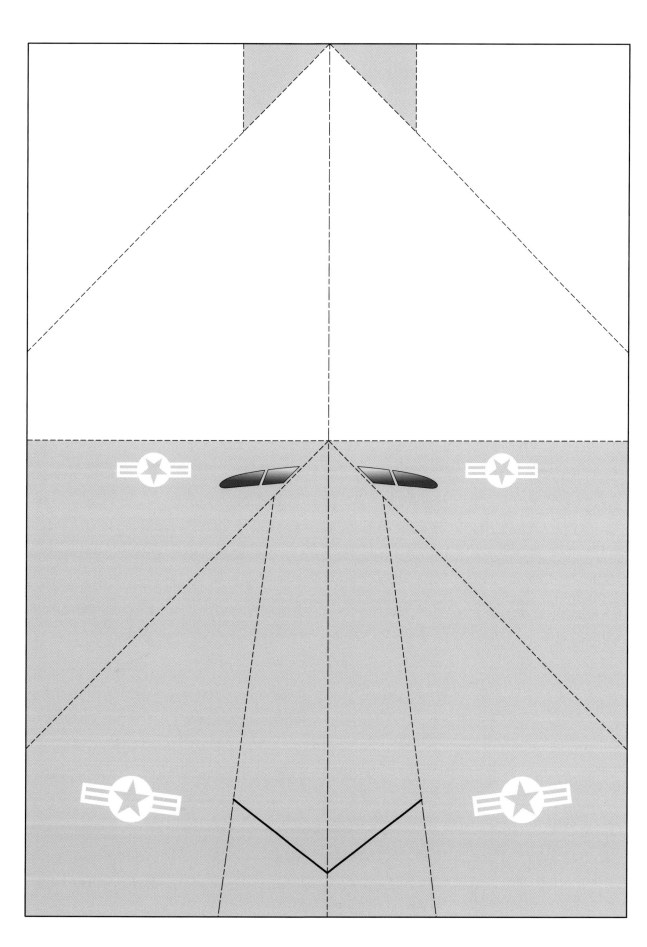

Divine Wind Racing Plane

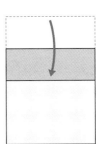

Take-off Tip

If necessary, curve up the rear edges of the wings between thumb and finger to achieve a smooth glide. Launch gently.

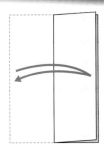

1. With the printed side facing up, fold the left edge to the right one, crease and then unfold.

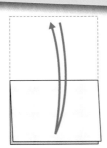

2. Fold the top edge down to the bottom one, crease and then unfold.

3. Flip over so printed side faces down and fold the top edge down to the centre crease.

4. Diagonally fold in the two top corners along the mountain fold lines.

5. Fold the top edge down along the mountain fold line.

6. Fold the plane in half.

7. Diagonally fold down the top corner and unfold. Repeat the fold the other way and unfold.

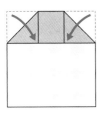

8. Take the front top edge, pull down and crease to shape.

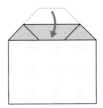

9. Fold back the rear top edge and crease well.

10. Fold down the wings.

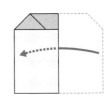

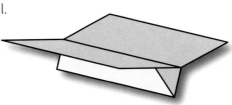

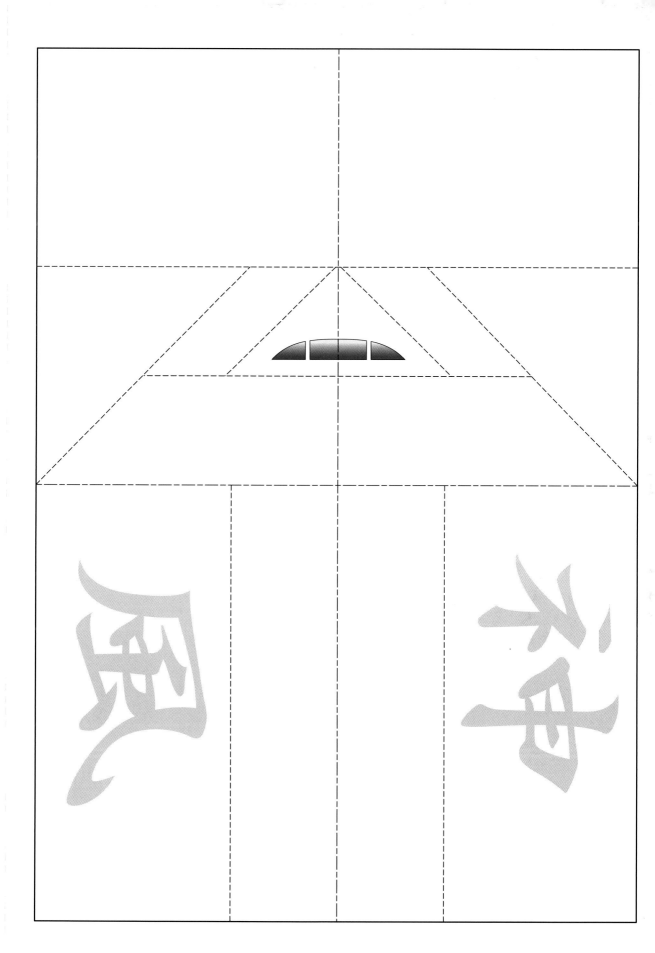

STEEL NEEDLE MISSLE

1. With the printed side facing up, fold the left edge to the right one, crease and then unfold.

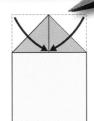

2. Flip over so printed side faces down and diagonally fold in the two top corners along the mountain fold lines.

3. Fold up the two corners along the valley fold lines and then unfold.

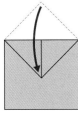

4. Flip the plane back and fold down the top point along the valley fold line.

5. Diagonally fold up the point to the top edge along the mountain fold line and then unfold.

6. Repeat step 5 along the other valley fold line and then unfold.

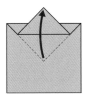

7. Fold up the point and crease along the mountain fold line.

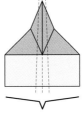

8. Flip the plane over. Fold the left corner diagonally inwards and the plane will fall into the shape shown on the right of the diagram. Repeat with the right corner.

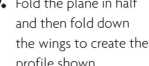

9. Fold the plane in half and then fold down the wings to create the profile shown.

TAKE-OFF TIP
If necessary, curve up the rear edges of the wings between thumb and finger to achieve a smooth glide. Launch gently.

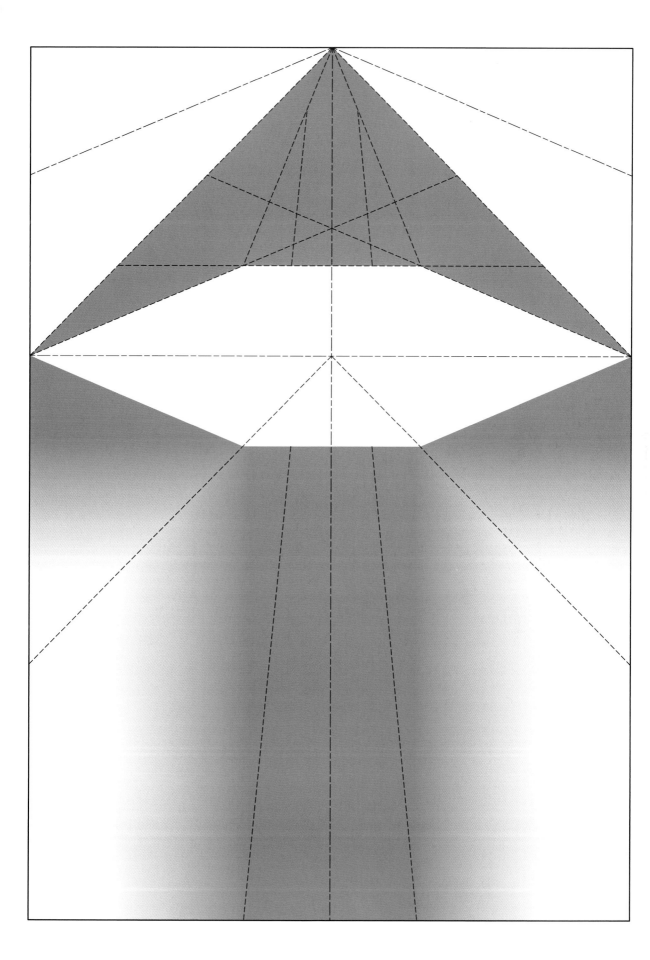

Delta Star Fighter

1.
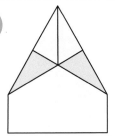
With the printed side facing up, fold the left edge to the right one, crease and then unfold.

2.
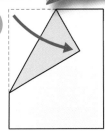
Flip over so printed side faces down and diagonally fold in the top left corner along the mountain fold line.

3.

Horizontally fold the point back to the left edge along the valley fold line.

4.
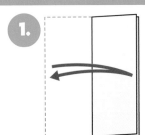
Repeat steps 2 and 3 with the top right corner. Your plane should now look like this.

5.
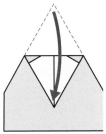
Flip over and fold down the top point along the mountain fold line.

6.
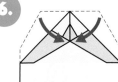
Flip the plan back over again and diagonally fold the two top corners down to the centre along the mountain fold lines.

7.
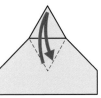
Flip the plane over and fold up the point, crease and then unfold.

8.

Lift up the two centre pockets, folding along the crease created in step 7 and collapse and crease to make the shape shown in step 9.

9.
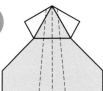
Fold the plane in half and then fold down the wings.

Take-off Tip
If necessary, curve up the rear edges of the wings between thumb and finger to achieve a smooth glide. Launch gently.

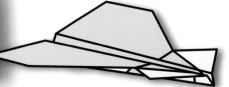

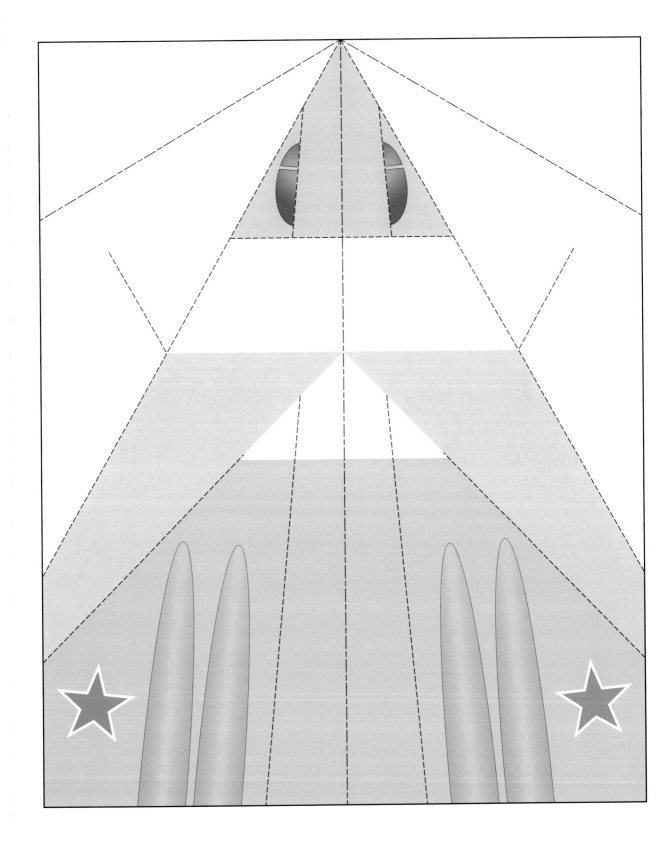

Firefly Space Shuttle

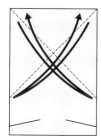

1. With the printed side face down, diagonally fold down the top left corner along the mountain fold line, crease and then unfold. Repeat with the right corner.

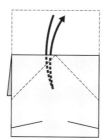

2. Fold the top edge back along the valley fold line and then unfold.

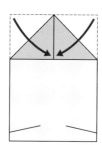

3. Fold the two top corners diagonally into the centre.

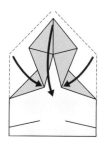

4. Fold the left and right points into the centre and fold down the top point to the same place.

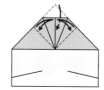

5. Fold back the tip along the longer of the two mountain fold lines. Fold up the two small flaps and then unfold.

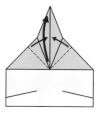

6. Pull up the central point and fold the small flaps into shape as shown.

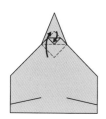

7. Flip over the plane and fold up the small flap, the fold down the smaller flap.

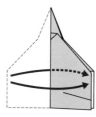

8. Fold the plane in half.

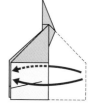

9. Fold down the wings. Use a small piece of sticky tape to hold the top of the 'cockpit' together. Curve up the two flaps at the rear of the wings and tape together.

Take-off Tip

Fold up the triangular wing elevators to achieve a smooth glide. Launch gently.

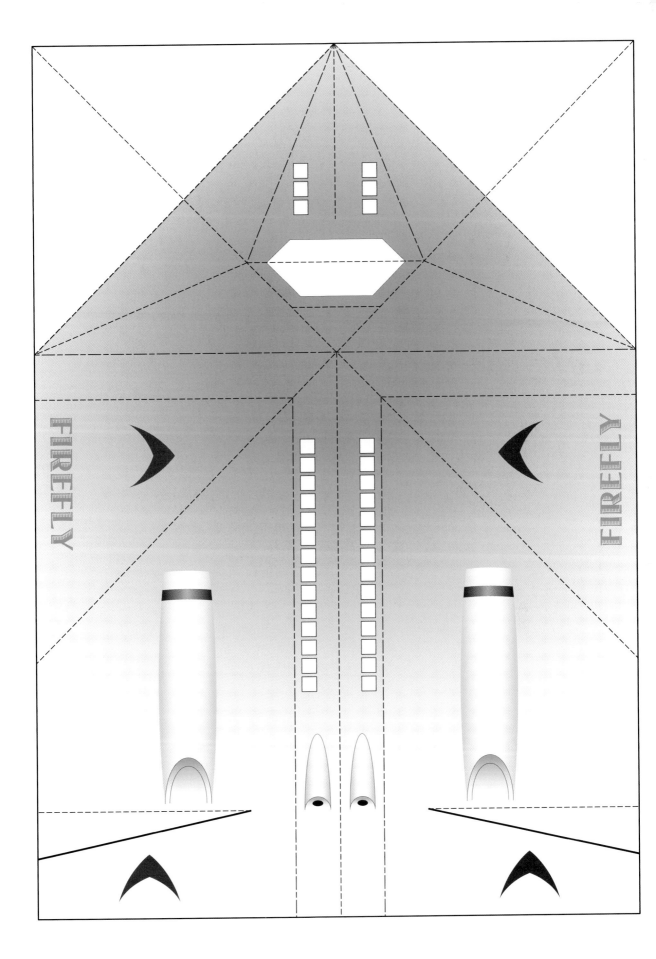

SPARROW STUNT FLYER

1. With the printed side up, fold down the top edge along the valley fold line and unfold.

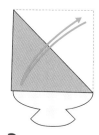

2. Flip over so printed side faces down and fold down the top right corner diagonally along the mountain fold line and unfold.

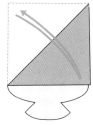

3. Repeat step 2 with the left top corner and unfold.

4. Push in the sides along the first fold and collapse to make the top a triangular shape.

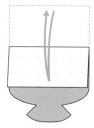

5. Take the left loose corner of the triangle and fold diagonally up to the top. Repeat with the right side.

6. Fold up the left corner of the new triangle and crease along the fold line and unfold. Repeat with the right side and unfold.

7. Fold down the left corner of the new triangle and crease along the fold line and unfold. Repeat with the right side and unfold.

8. Crease the small folds between those just created and pinch, press down and crease the folds.

9. Fold back the top tip and crease along the fold line.

10. Fold in half and crease everything well.

TAKE-OFF TIP
If necessary, curve up the rear edges of the tail between thumb and finger to fly in a loop. Launch forcefully.

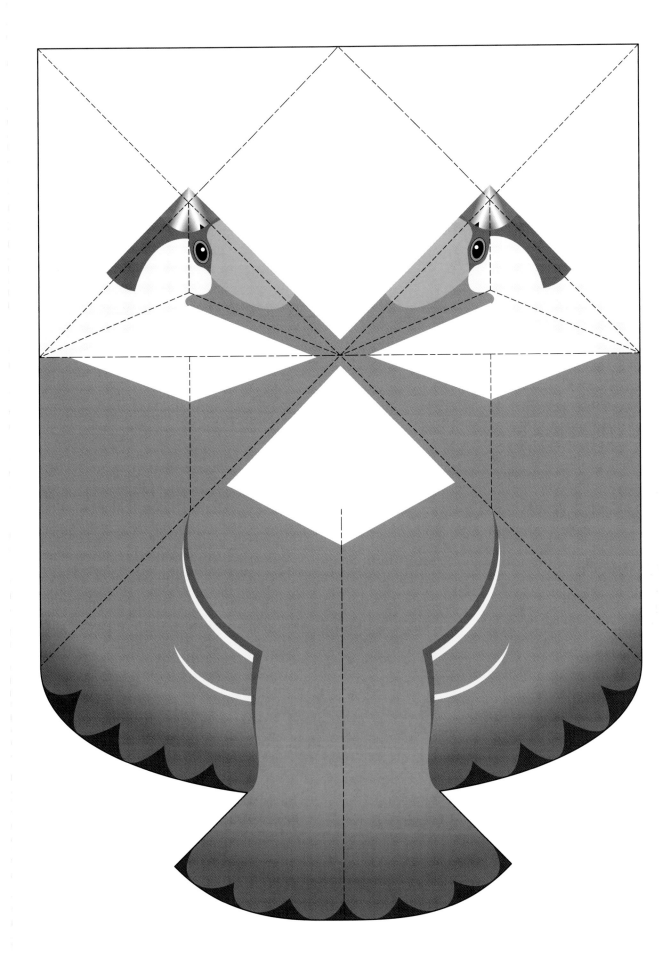

Unicorn Record Breaker

1.

Cut the 'V' shape that will later form the tail fin. With the printed side facing up fold the left edge to the right one, crease and then unfold.

2.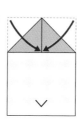

Flip over so printed side faces down and diagonally fold in the two top corners along the mountain fold lines.

3.

Fold up the two corners along the valley fold lines and then unfold.

4.

Flip the plane back and fold down the top point along the valley fold line.

5.

Diagonally fold up the point to the top edge along the mountain fold line and then unfold.

6.

Repeat step 5 along the other valley fold line and then unfold.

7.

Fold up the point and crease along the mountain fold line.

8.

Flip the plane over. Fold the left corner diagonally inwards and the plane will fall into the shape shown on the right of the diagram. Repeat with the right corner.

9.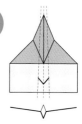

Fold the plane in half and then fold down the wings to create the profile shown. Push up the tail fin.

Take-off Tip
If necessary, curve up the rear edges of the wings between thumb and finger to achieve a smooth glide. Launch gently.

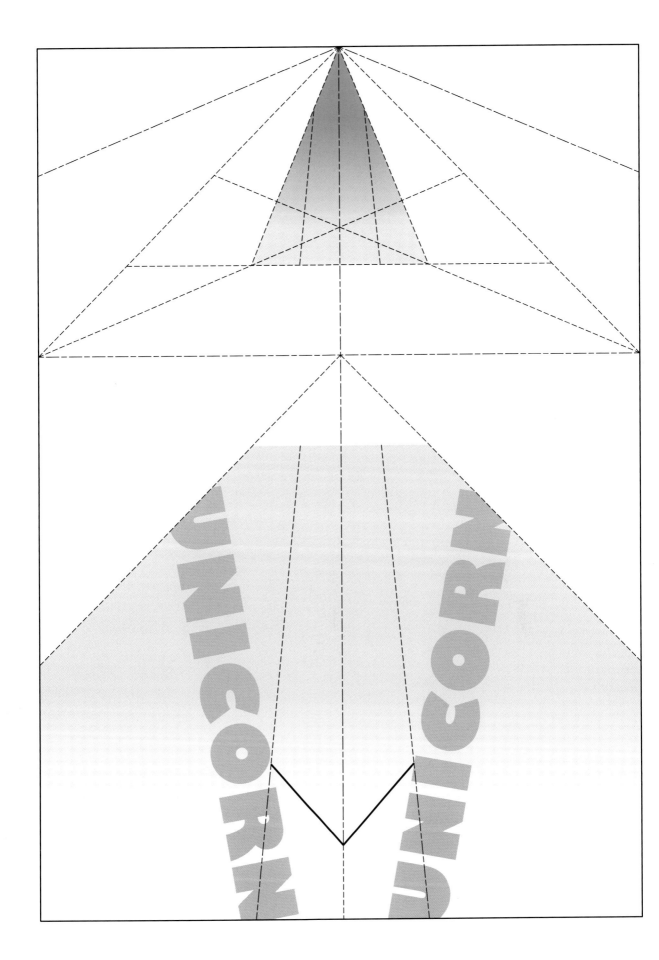

Desert Storm Fighter

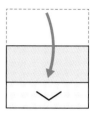

Take-off Tip
If necessary, curve up the rear edges of the wings between thumb and finger to achieve a smooth glide. Launch gently.

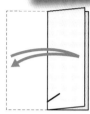

1. Cut the 'V' shape that will later form the tail fin. With the printed side facing up, fold the left edge to the right one, crease and then unfold.

2. Flip over so printed side faces down and diagonally fold in the top left corner along the mountain fold line, then unfold.

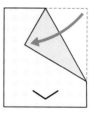

3. Repeat step 2 with the top right corner.

4. Fold down the top edge along the mountain fold line.

5. Diagonally fold the top two corners along the mountain fold lines, crease and then unfold. Fold again but this time fold back, crease and and then unfold.

6. Take the left corner of the front fold and position along the top edge as shown and crease to the new shape.

7. Repeat step 6 with the right corner of the front fold.

8. Your plane should now look like this.

9. Diagonally fold the top left point down along the mountain fold line.

10. Fold up the middle point and crease well.

11. Fold the plane in half.

12. Fold down the wings and push up the tail fin.

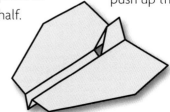

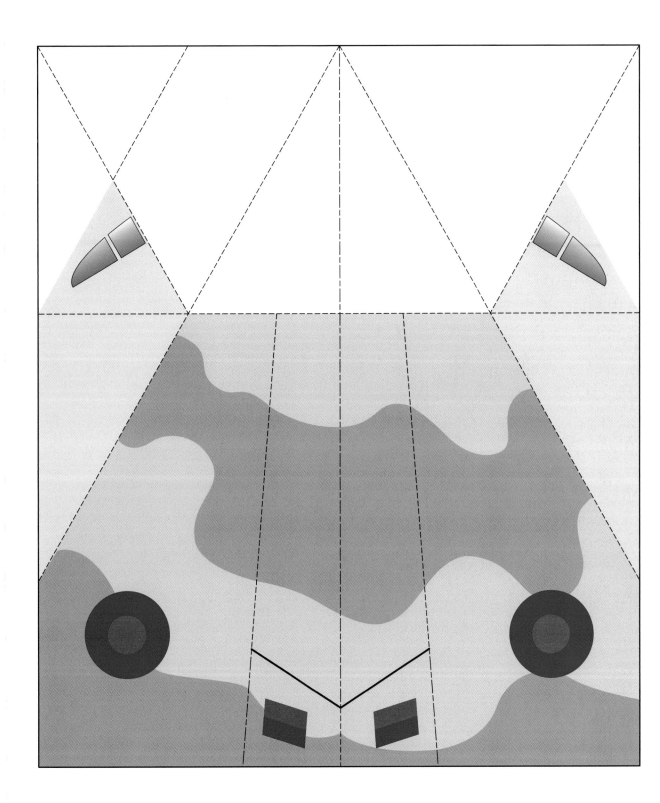

DRONE RECONNAISSANCE AIRCRAFT

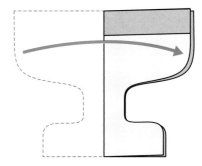

1. Lay the plane face down and fold the top edge down 5 times.

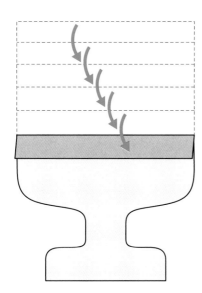

2. Flip the plane over and fold the plane in half.

3. Fold up the tail wing tips to make the profile as shown.

TAKE-OFF TIP
If necessary, curve up the rear edges of the wings between thumb and finger to achieve a smooth glide. Launch gently.

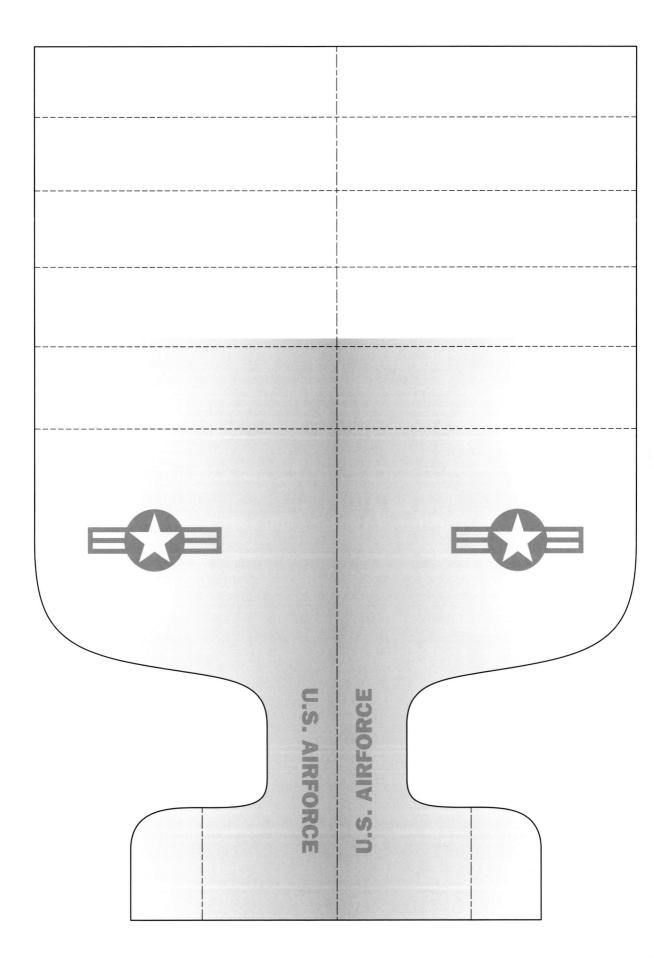

U.S. AIRFORCE

U.S. AIRFORCE

SYCAMORE HELICOPTER

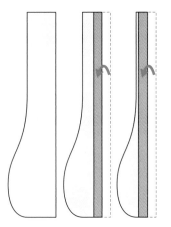

Cut out the shape and lay printed side down. Fold the long straight edge once and then twice.

2.

From the end fold over 6 times.

3.

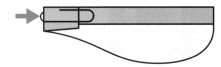

Push a paper clip into place to hold it together.

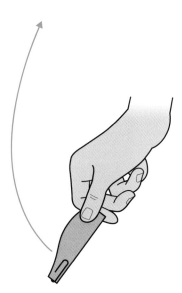

Take-off Tip
To launch, hold at the wide end and throw hard up into the air as shown.

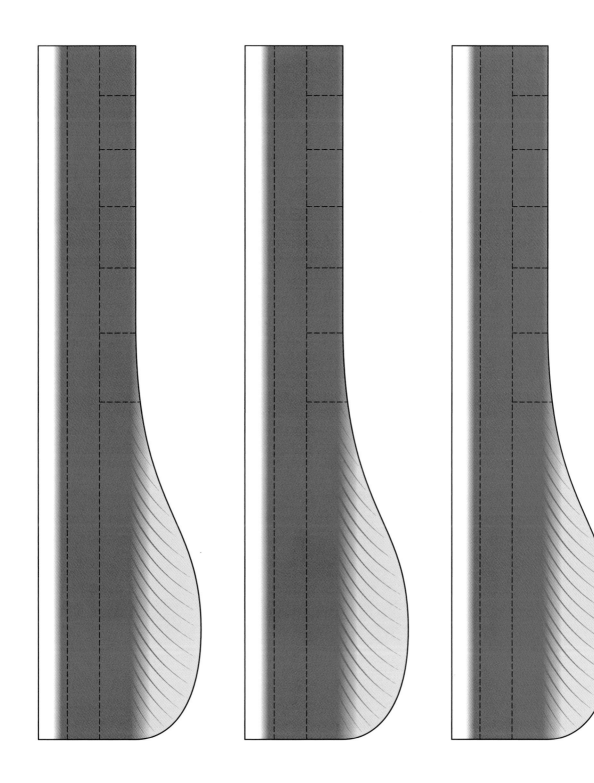

Kaleidokite Kite

1. Lay the kite face down, fold in half diagonally and then unfold.

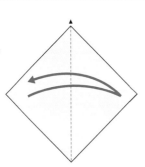

2. Flip the kite over and fold the top two edges to the centre.

3. Diagonally fold the points upwards along the mountain fold lines.

4. Join the 4 pieces of tail together with sticky tape.

5. Tie the tail to the bottom of the kite with button thread. Tie a 3-foot (1 metre) length of button thread through holes made at the dots on each side to make a bridle. Hold the two holes together between finger and thumb of one hand and find the centre point of the bridle and tie a loop. Tie more thread to this loop for a kite line.

Take-off Tip
Fly in a gentle wind.

SWALLOW STUNT FLYER

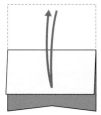

1. With the sheet laying face upwards, fold down the top edge along the valley fold line, and then unfold.

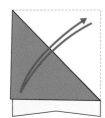

2. Flip the sheet over and diagonally fold the top right corner down to left side along the mountain fold line, and then unfold.

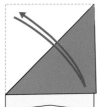

3. Repeat step 2 with the top left corner and unfold.

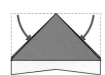

4. Push in the sides along the first fold and collapse to make the top a triangular shape.

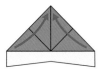

5. Take the left loose corner of the triangle and fold diagonally up to the top. Repeat with the right side.

6. Fold up the left corner of the new triangle and crease along the fold line and unfold. Repeat with the right side and unfold.

7. Fold down the left corner of the new triangle and crease along the fold line and unfold. Repeat with the right side and unfold.

8. Crease the small folds between those just created and pinch, press down and crease the folds.

9. Cut out the tail and fold down the two top corners.

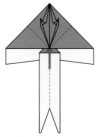

10. Push the tail into the plane so the point fits into the nose.

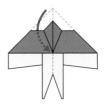

11. Fold the nose over and crease well.

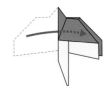

12. Fold the plane in half.

TAKE-OFF TIP
If necessary, curve up the rear edges of the tail between thumb and finger to fly in a loop. Launch forcefully.

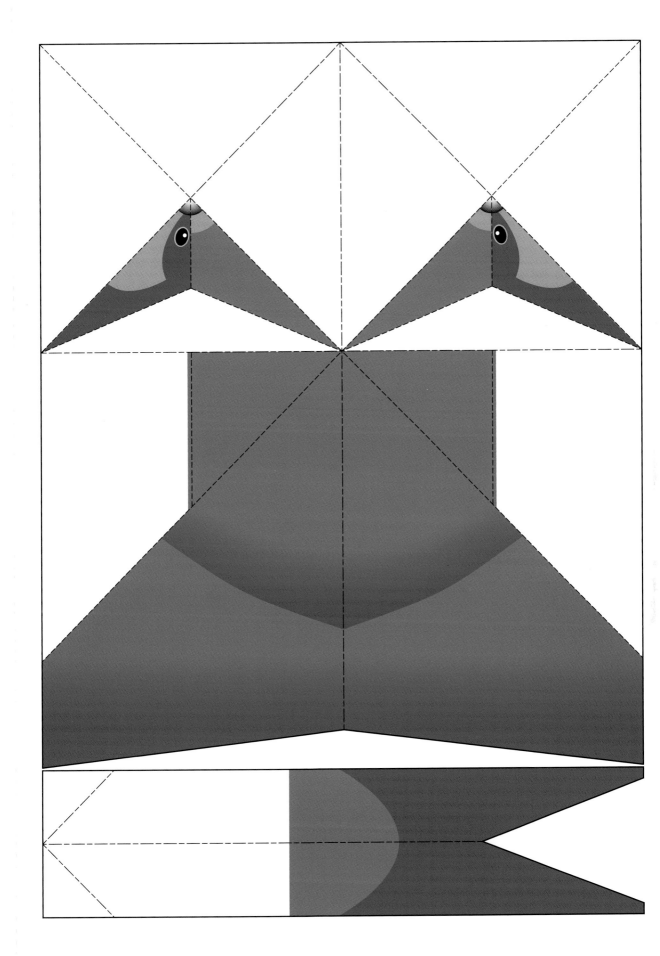

Rapier Racing Plane

1.

With the printed side face down, fold in half and then unfold.

2.

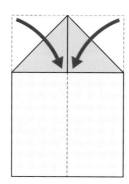

Fold the top left corner into the central crease. Repeat with the right corner.

3.

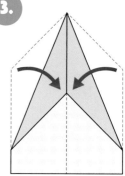

Fold the top left edge into the central crease. Repeat with the right edge.

4.

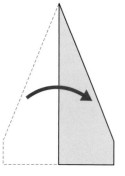

Valley fold the plane in half.

5.

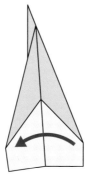

Fold down the wings and fold up the rear elevators slightly.

Take-off Tip
Adjust the elevators to achieve a smooth glide. Launch gently.

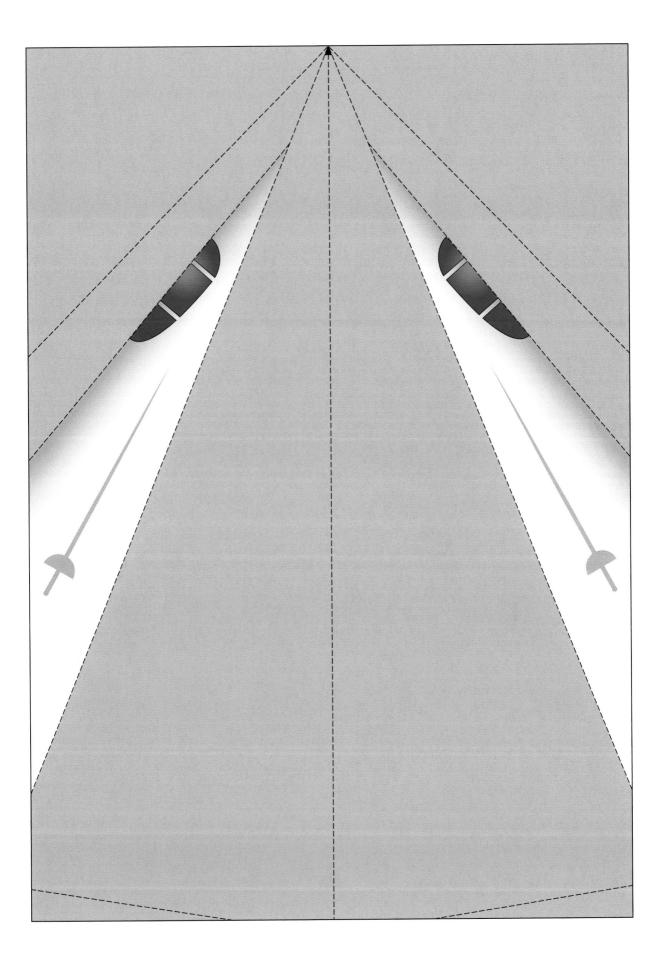

Aurora High Speed Aircraft

1. With the printed side up fold in half and unfold.

2. Flip over so printed side faces down and diagonally fold down the top left and right corners to to the centre fold.

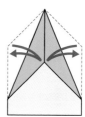

3. Fold the new side points into the centre along the mountain fold lines, crease and then unfold.

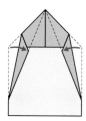

4. Fold the two points to the crease line created in step 3 along the mountain fold lines.

5. Fold the sides in along the creases created in step 3.

6. Flip the plane over and fold the top point down along the mountain fold line.

7. Fold the point up along the fold line.

8. Fold in half.

9. Fold down the wings along the mountain fold lines. Use a small piece of sticky tape across the front to keep the two sides of the body together.

Take-off Tip
If necessary, curve the rear edges of the wings and tail between thumb and finger to achieve a smooth glide. Launch gently.

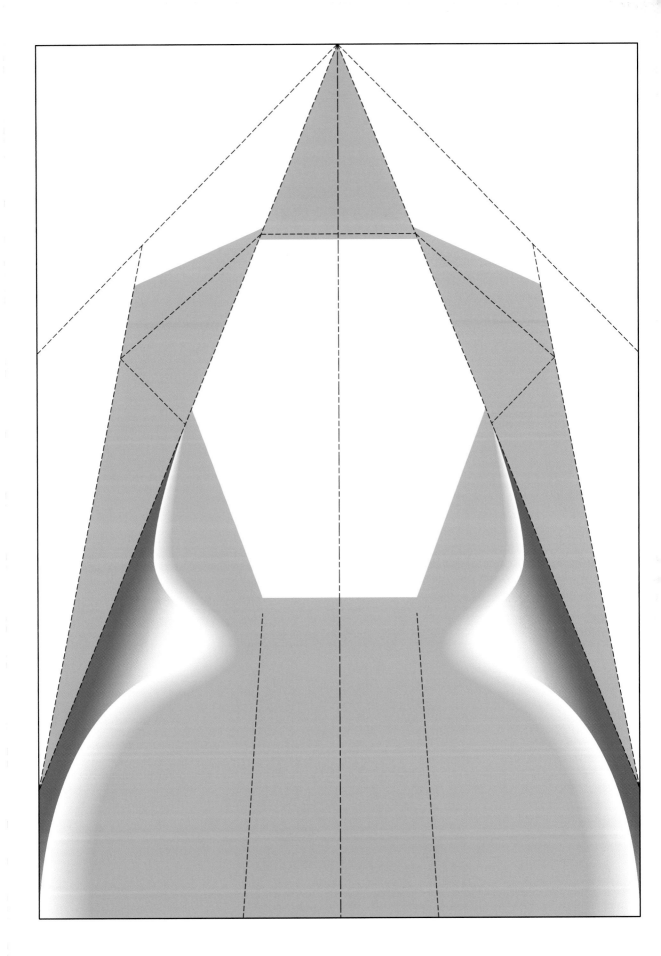

APACHE FIGHTER

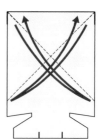

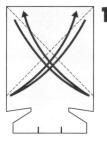

1. Make the two small cuts for the elevators. With the printed side face down diagonally fold down, the top left corner along the mountain fold line, crease and then unfold. Repeat with the right corner.

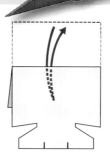

2. Fold the top edge back along the valley fold line and then unfold.

3. Fold the two top corners diagonally into the centre.

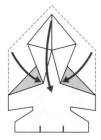

4. Fold the left and right points into the centre and fold down the top point to the same place.

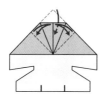

5. Fold back the tip along the longer of the 2 mountain fold lines. Fold up the 2 small flaps and then unfold.

6. Pull up the central point and fold the small flaps into shape as shown.

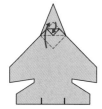

7. Flip over the plane and fold up the small flap, then fold down the smaller flap.

8. Fold the plane in half.

9. Fold down the wings. Use a small piece of sticky tape to hold the top of the 'cockpit' together.

TAKE-OFF TIP
Fold up the rear elevators to achieve a smooth glide. Launch gently.

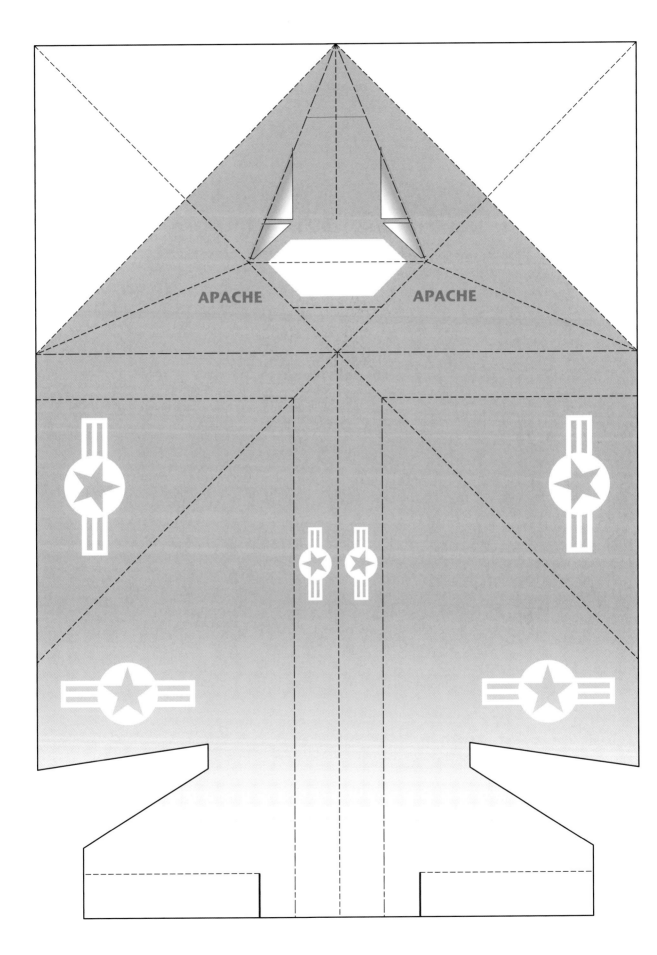

Hawk Moth Flyer

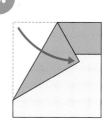

1.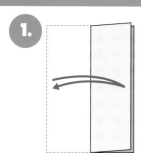

With the printed side up, fold in half and unfold.

2.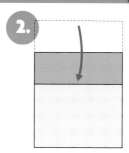

Flip over so printed side faces down and fold down the top along the mountain fold line.

3.

Diagonally fold the top left point along the mountain fold line.

4.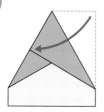

Diagonally fold the top right point along the mountain fold line.

5.

Fold down the top point along the mountain fold line, crease and then unfold.

6.

Fold the left point, created in step 4, to the centre along the fold line, crease and then unfold.

7.

Now fold down the top point again and push the tab formed in step 6 into the pocket in its side.

8.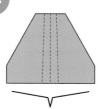

Fold the plane in half and then fold down the wings to form the profile shown.

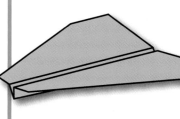

Take-off Tip
If necessary, curve up the rear edges of the wings between thumb and finger to achieve a smooth glide. Launch gently.

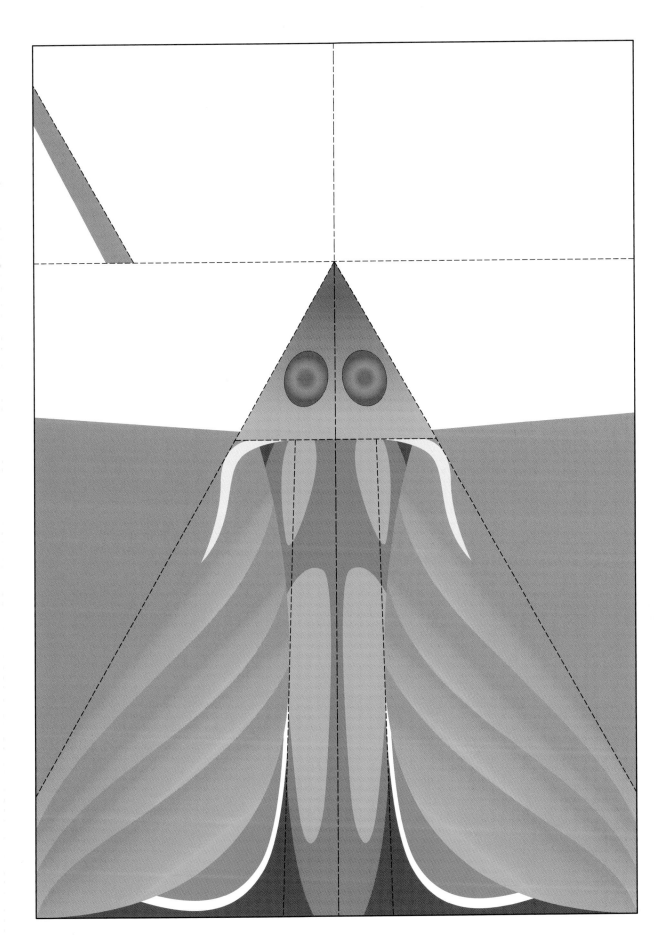

Red Ark Airliner

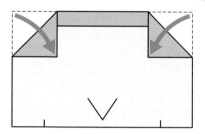

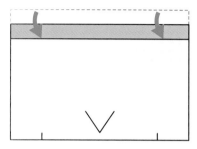

1. Cut the 'V' shape that will later form the tail fin and the two small cuts for the elevators. With the printed side face down, fold down the long top edge along the mountain fold line.

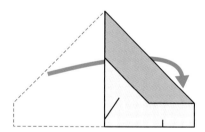

2. Diagonally fold down the top left corner along the mountain fold line and repeat with the right side.

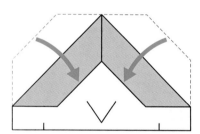

3. Fold the new top edges diagonally along the mountain fold lines.

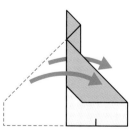

4. Fold the plane in half.

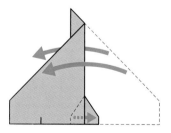

5. Fold the sides down and push up the tail fin.

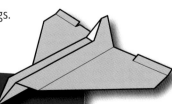

6. Fold up the wings.

Take-off Tip
Fold up the rear elevators to achieve a smooth glide. Launch gently.

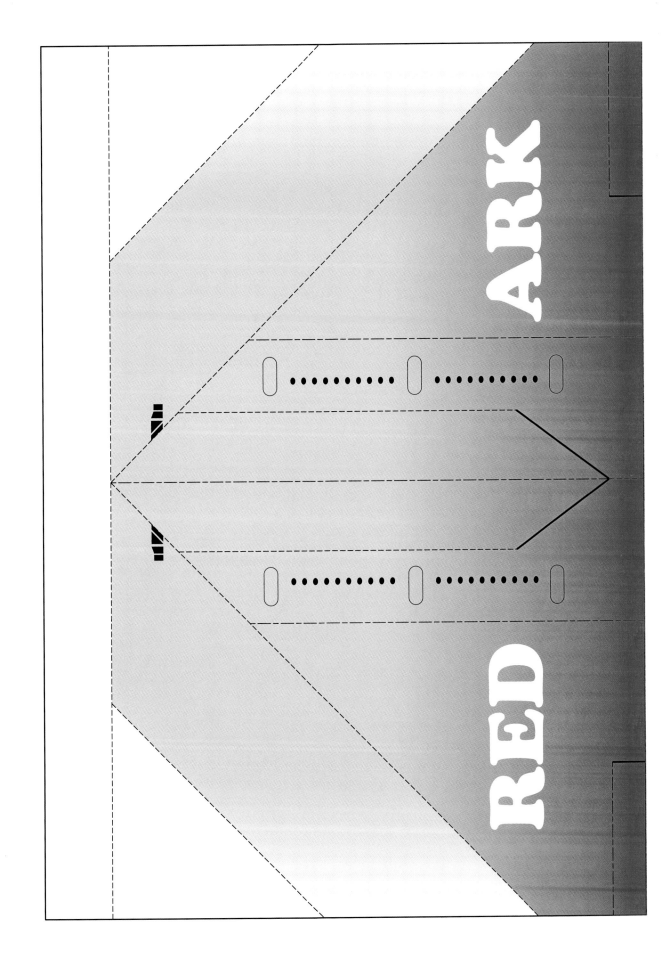

ORION BOMBER

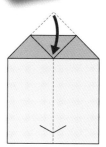

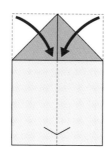

1. Cut the 'V' shape that will later form the tail fin. With the printed side face up, fold in half and then unfold.

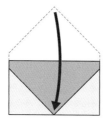

2. Flip over so printed side faces down and diagonally fold in the two top corners to the centre.

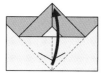

3. Fold down the top tip along the mountain fold line.

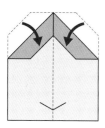

4. Fold down the two new top edges along the mountain fold lines.

5. Fold down the top tip to line up with the bottom edge.

6. Fold up the tip and crease along the mountain fold line.

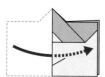

7. Fold the plane in half.

8. Fold down the wings and fold up the wing tips. Push up the tail fin.

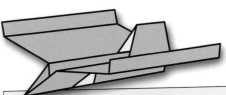

TAKE-OFF TIP
If necessary, curve up the rear edges of the wings between thumb and finger to achieve a smooth glide. Launch gently.

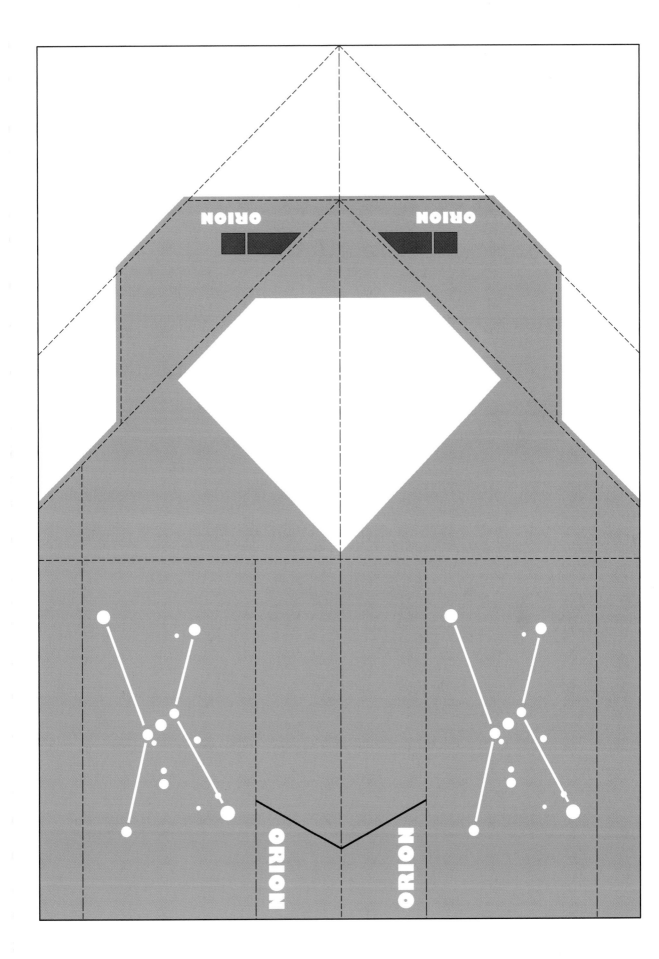

Swift Glider

1.

With the printed side facing down fold the left edge to the right one, crease and unfold.

2.

Diagonally fold down the top left corner along the mountain fold line.

3.

Valley fold the point to the left along the fold line.

4.

Repeat steps 2 and 3 with the right side of the plane. Your plane should now look like this.

5.

Fold down the top point 3 times along the fold lines.

6.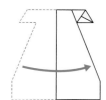

Fold the model in half.

7.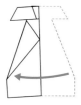

Fold down both wings. Stick the front edges of the fuselage together with a small piece of sticky tape.

Take-off Tip
If necessary, curve up the rear edges of the wings between thumb and finger to achieve a smooth glide. Launch gently.

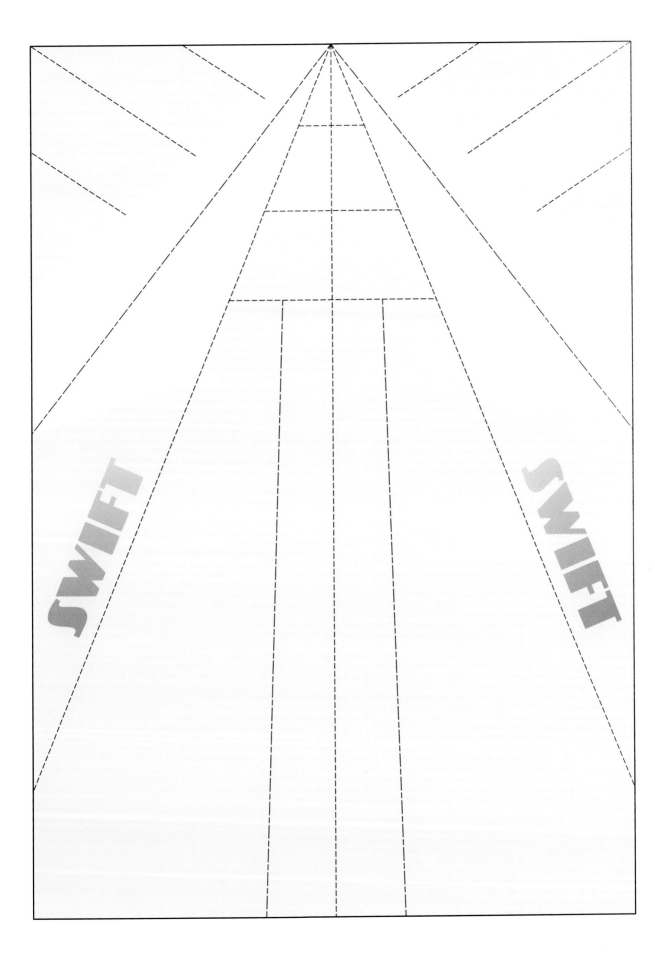

Viper Ground Attack Aircraft

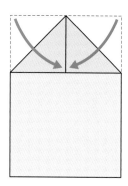

1. With the printed side face down, fold in the top two corners to the centre.

2. Fold down the top point along the mountain fold line.

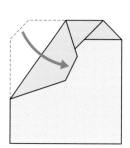

3. Diagonally fold down the top left edge and crease along the mountain fold line.

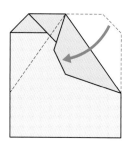

4. Fold back the flap created in step 3 and repeat with the right side.

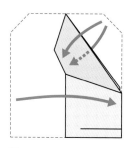

5. Flip the plane over and fold it in half. Then fold down the flaps created in stages 3 and 4.

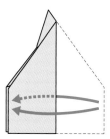

6. Fold down the wings and fold up the wing tips.

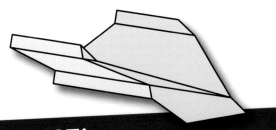

Take-off Tip
If necessary, curve up the rear edges of the wings between thumb and finger to achieve a smooth glide. Launch gently.

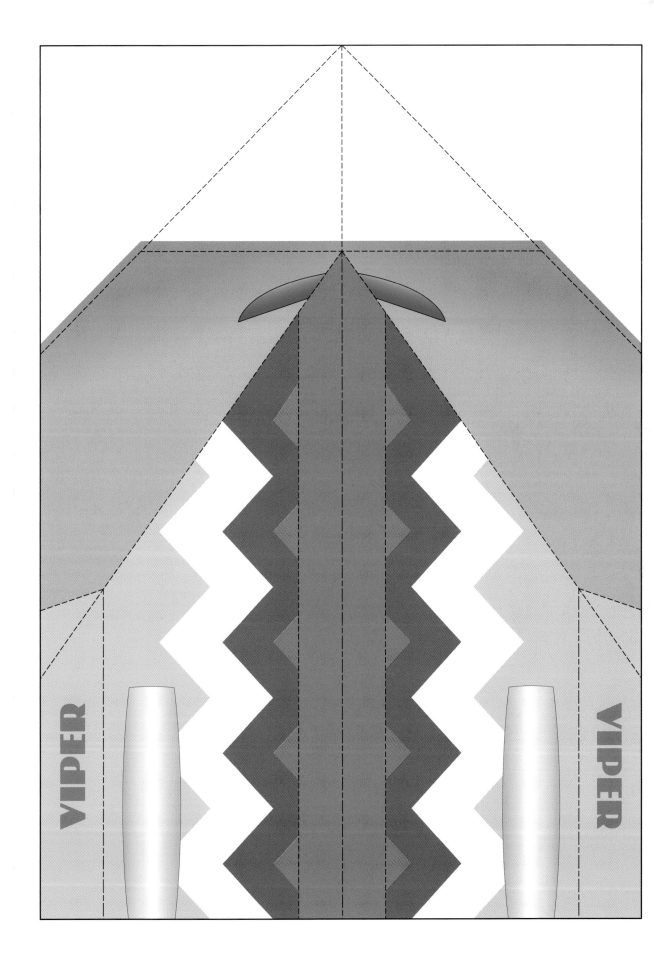

TYPHOON FIGHTER

1. With the printed side face up, fold in half and then unfold.

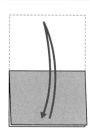

2. Flip over so printed side faces down and fold down the top edge to the bottom edge and unfold.

3. Fold down the top edge to the crease created in step 2.

4. Diagonally fold the top left corner down to the centre and then unfold. Repeat with the top right corner.

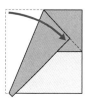

5. Fold down the top left edge to line up with the diagonal crease created on the right in step 4.

6. Horizontally fold the point across to the left. Repeat steps 5 and 6 with the top right point.

7. Fold down the top point along the mountain fold line.

8. Fold up the point along the mountain fold line.

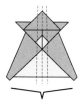

9. Fold in half and then fold down the wings to match the profile in the diagram.

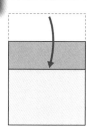

TAKE-OFF TIP
If necessary, curve up the rear edges of the wings between thumb and finger to achieve a smooth glide. Launch gently.

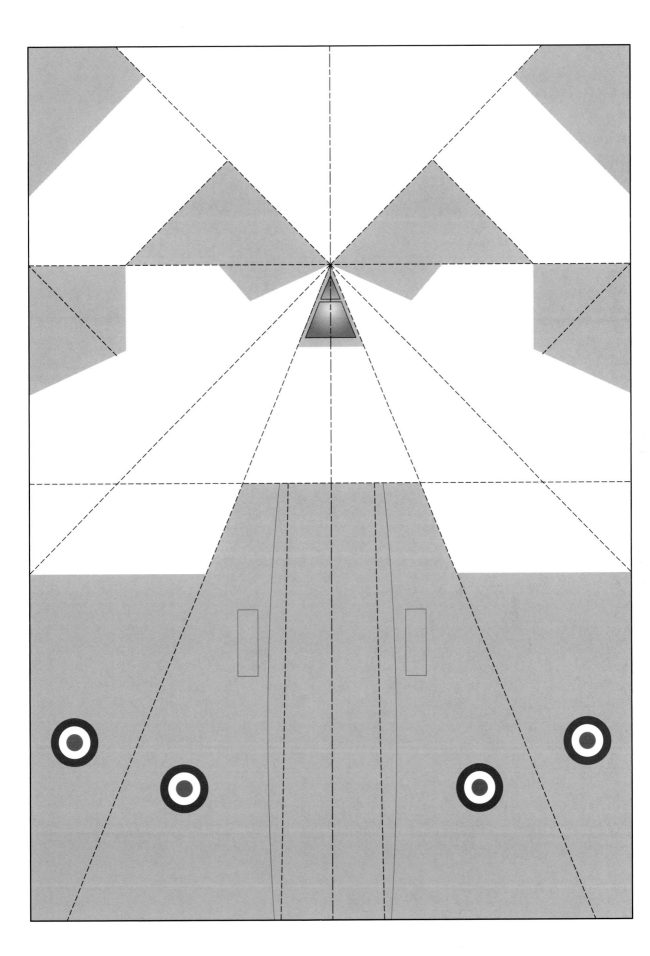

Andromeda Spacecraft

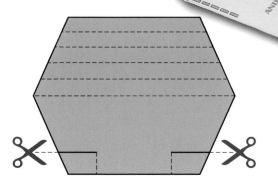

Cut the two slots that will later form the tail fins.

Flip over so printed side faces down and fold down the top edge five times. Crease well.

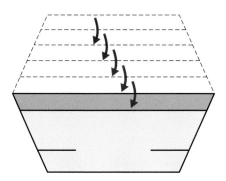

Fold the plane in half. Open up to form a dihedral and fold up the two tail fins.

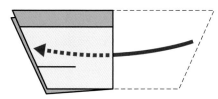

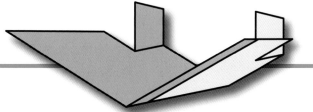

Take-off Tip
Launch very gently.

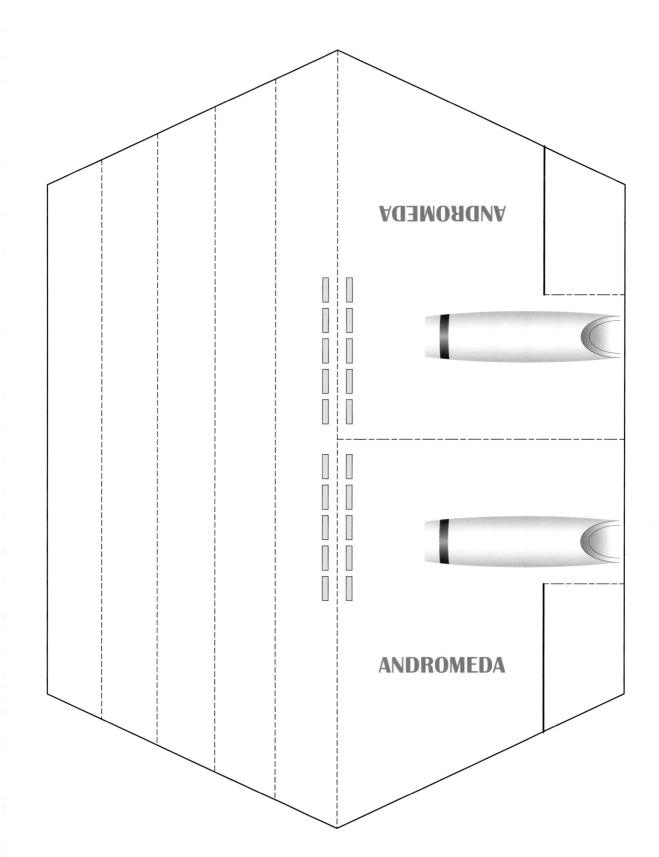

Charger Racing Plane

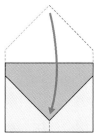

1. With the printed side facing up, fold the left edge to the right one, crease and then unfold.

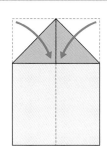

2. Fold in the two top corners along the mountain fold lines.

3. Fold down the top point along the mountain fold line.

4. Fold in the two top corners along the mountain fold lines.

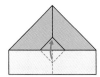

5. Fold up the small pointed tab along the fold line.

6. Fold the plane in half.

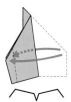

7. Fold down the wings and fold down the wing tips to create the profile shown.

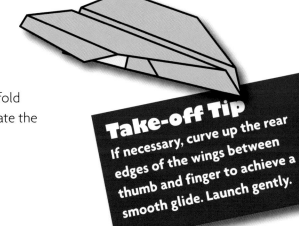

Take-off Tip
If necessary, curve up the rear edges of the wings between thumb and finger to achieve a smooth glide. Launch gently.

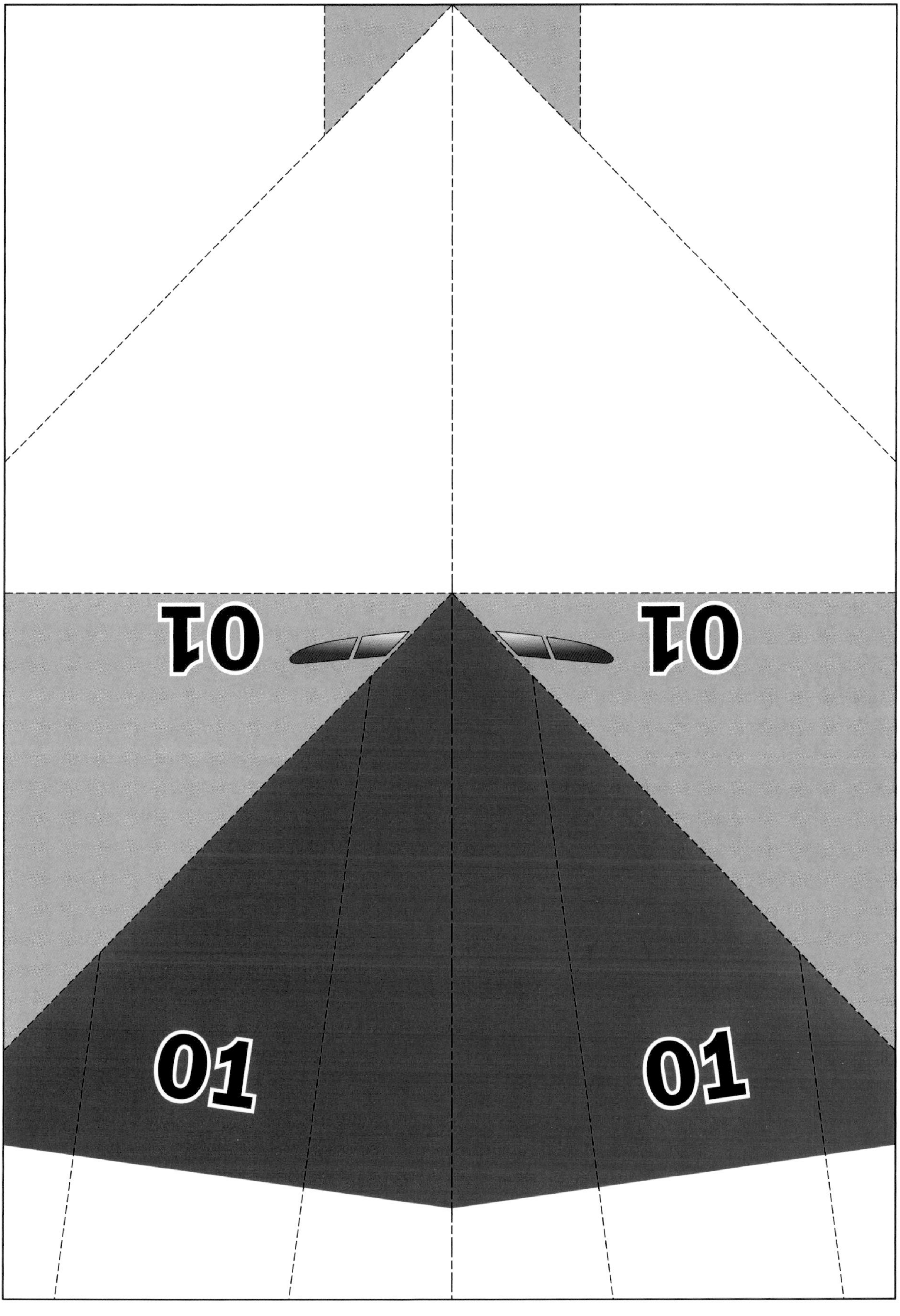
01
01
01
01

FIREFLY HELICOPTER

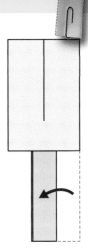

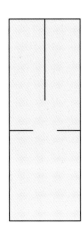

1. Cut out a helicopter and make the three extra cuts a s shown.

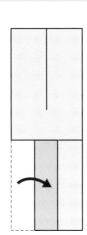

2. With the helicopter printed side down, fold the bottom left edge across along the mountain fold line.

3. Repeat step 2 with the bottom right edge.

4. Push on a paper clip.

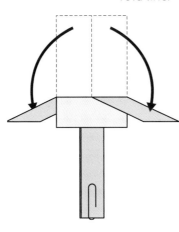

5. Fold down the two top flaps, one forward and the other behind.

TAKE-OFF TIP
Launch gently. Adjust the elevators to achieve a smooth glide.

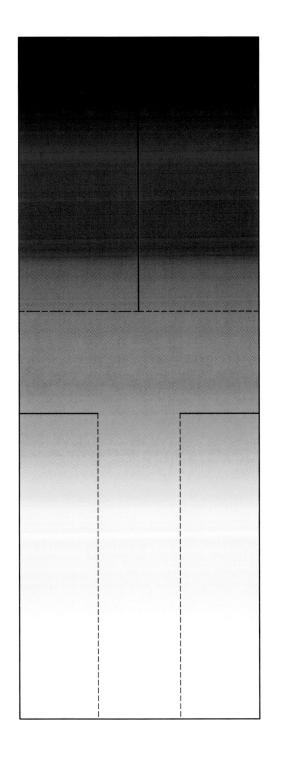

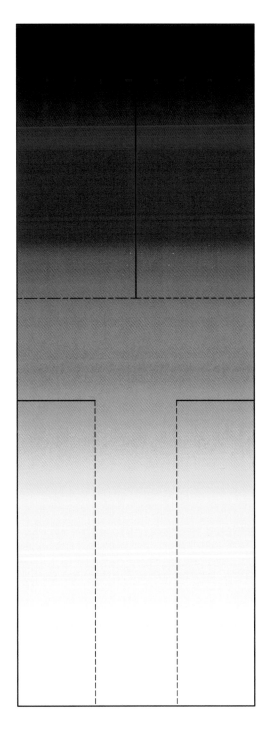

Space Explorer

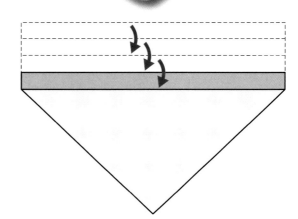

Lay the plane printed side down and fold down the top edge three times along the mountain fold lines. Crease well.

2.

Tape together the two ends of the folded section to produce a smooth cylinder shape.

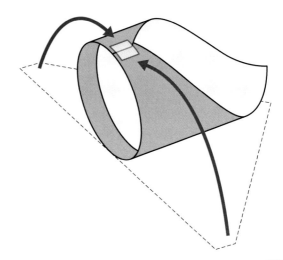

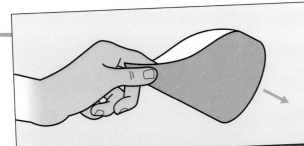

Take-off Tip

Launch by holding the point at the rear and gently pushing away and releasing the plane.

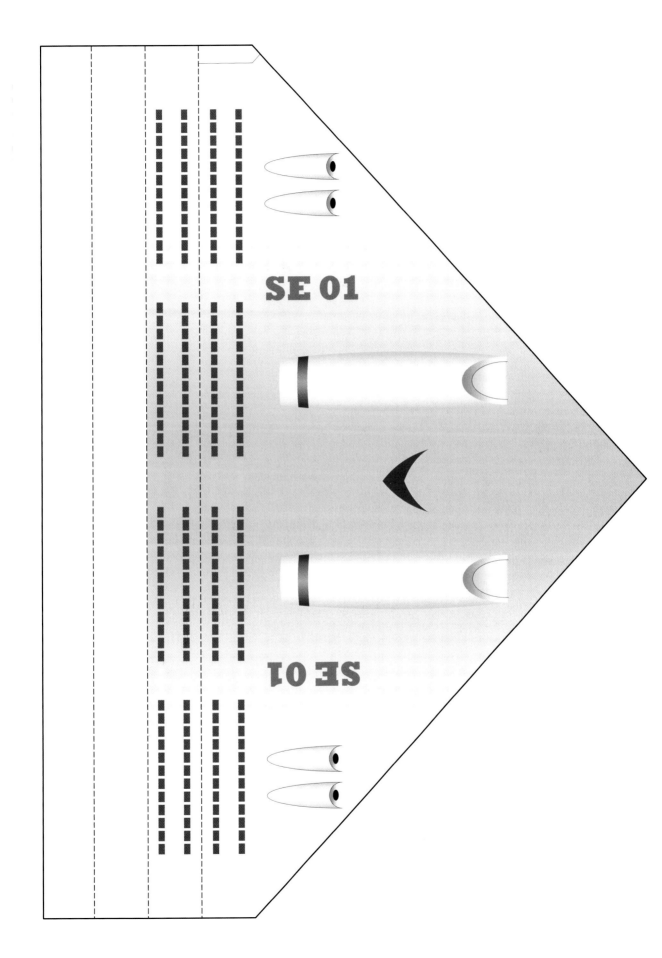

Buzzard Glider

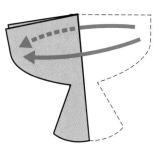

1. With the printed side face down, fold in the top two corners to the centre.

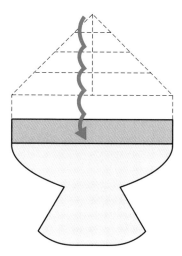

2. Fold down five times.

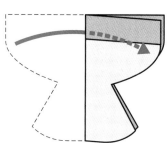

3. Flip over so printed side faces up and fold in half.

4. Fold down the wings.

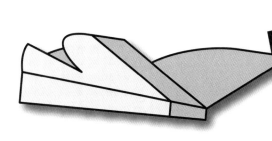

Take-off Tip

If necessary, curve up the rear edges of the wings and tail between thumb and finger to achieve a smooth glide. Launch gently.

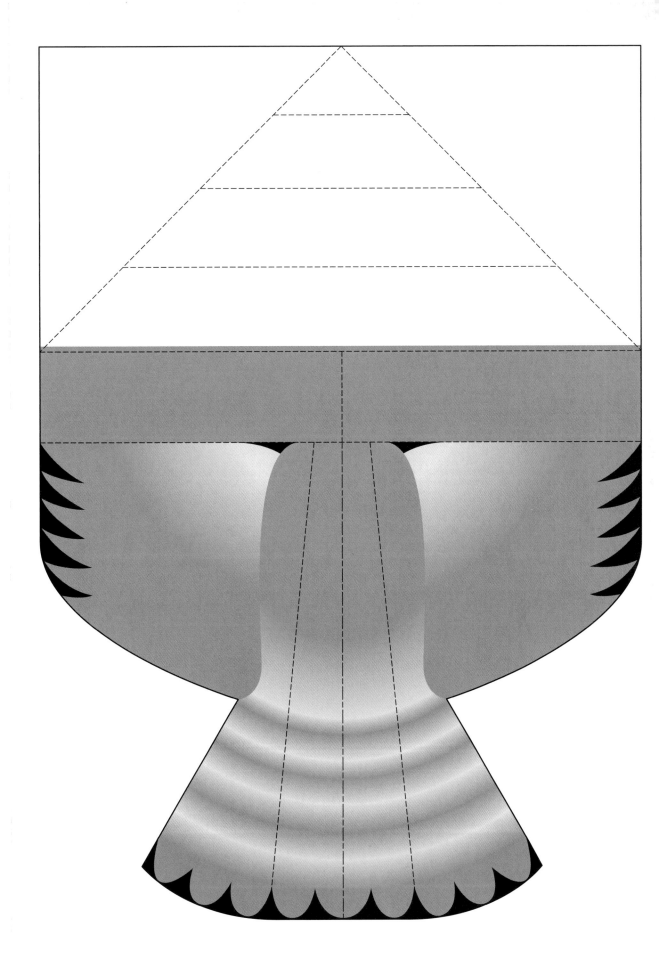

GIGANTOR BOMBER

1. With the printed side facing up, fold the left edge to the right one, crease and unfold.

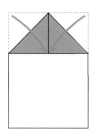

2. Diagonally fold down the top left and right corners along the mountain fold lines.

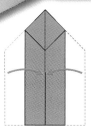

3. Fold the left and right edges into the centre crease.

4. Diagonally fold down top left edge along the fold line, crease and unfold.

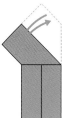

5. Repeat step 4 with the top right edge, crease and unfold.

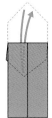

6. Fold back the top point along the mountain fold line, crease and unfold.

7. Fold the left and right edges into the centre and collapse down the top point to the same place.

8. Unfold step 7 and crease along the horizontal mountain fold line. Refold and tuck the new flap into the pocket created in step 7.

9. Diagonally fold out and crease the 2 bottom inner points along the valley fold lines.

TAKE-OFF TIP
Curve up the rear edges of the wings between thumb and finger to achieve a smooth glide. Launch gently.

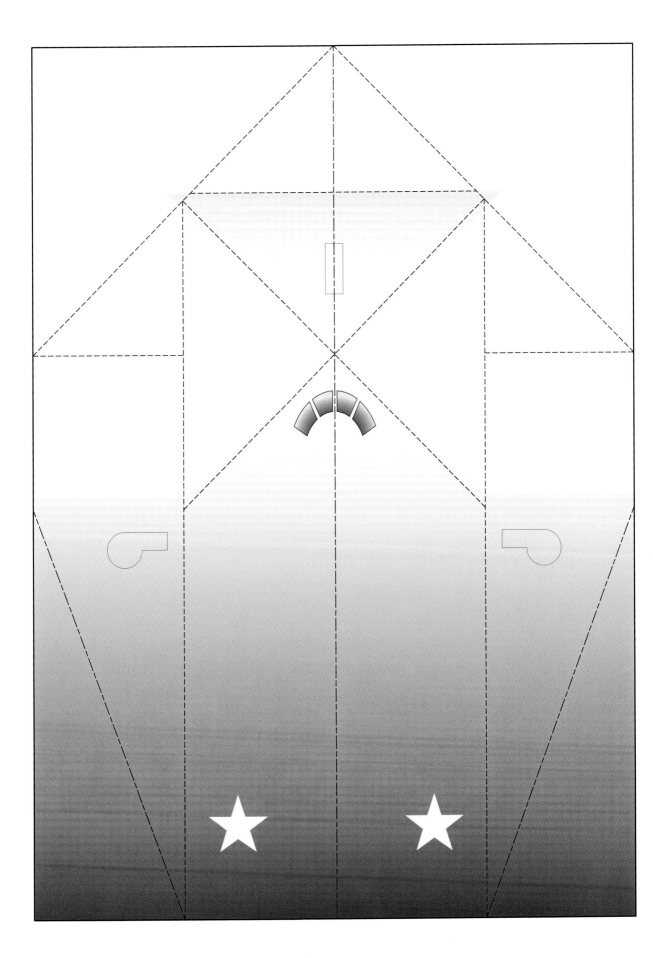

Baby Boomerangs

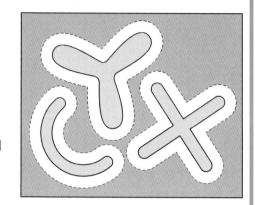

1.

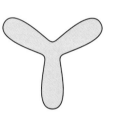

Cut out the boomerangs roughly around the dotted lines. Glue to some cardboard (an empty cereal packet is ideal).

2.

When dry cut out the boomerangs accurately.

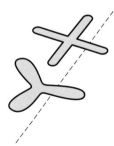

Take-off Tip
Lay them on a book with a short part of one of the arms sticking out as in the diagram. Hit smartly with a pencil.

Hammerhead Glider

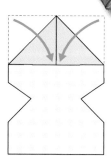

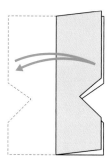

1. With the printed side facing up, fold the left edge to the right one, crease and unfold.

2. Flip the plane over and diagonally fold down the top left and right corners along the mountain fold lines.

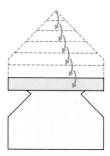

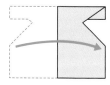

3. Fold down the top point six times along the mountain fold lines.

4. Fold the plane in half.

5. Fold back the wings.

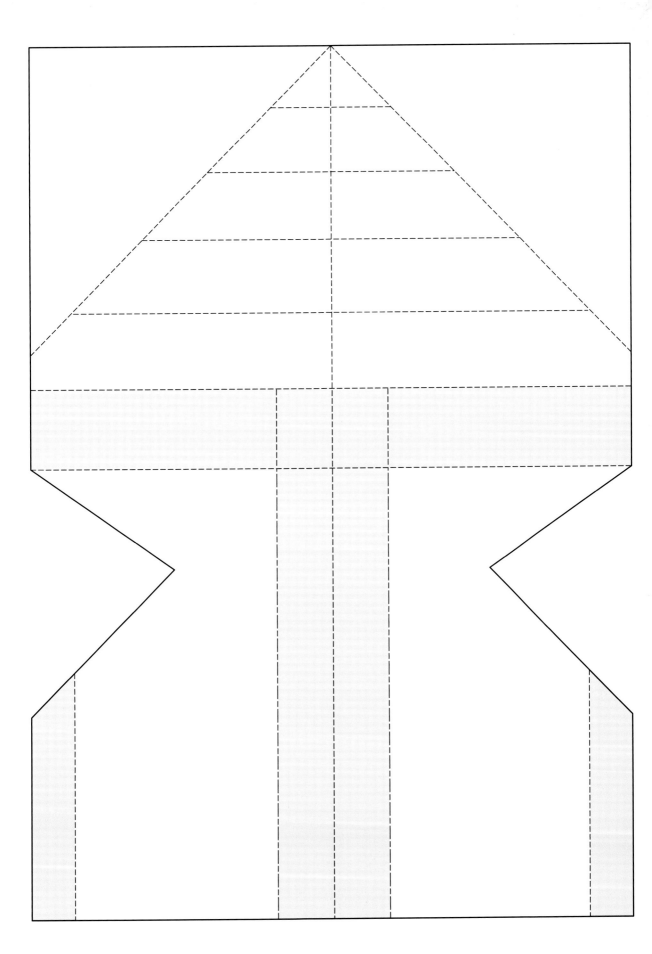

LIGHTNING FIGHTER

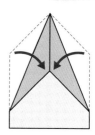

1. With the printed side up, fold in half and unfold.

2. Flip over so printed side faces down and diagonally fold down the top left and right corners to the centre fold.

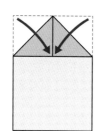

3. Fold the new side points into the centre along the mountain fold lines.

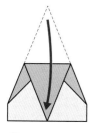

4. Fold down the top point to the bottom edge.

5. Fold down the two new top points along the mountain fold lines.

6. Fold up the bottom point along the mountain fold line.

7. Fold the plane in half.

8. Fold the wings down and fold up the flaps.

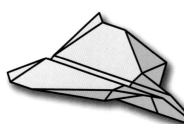

TAKE-OFF TIP
Adjust the flaps to achieve a smooth glide. Launch gently.

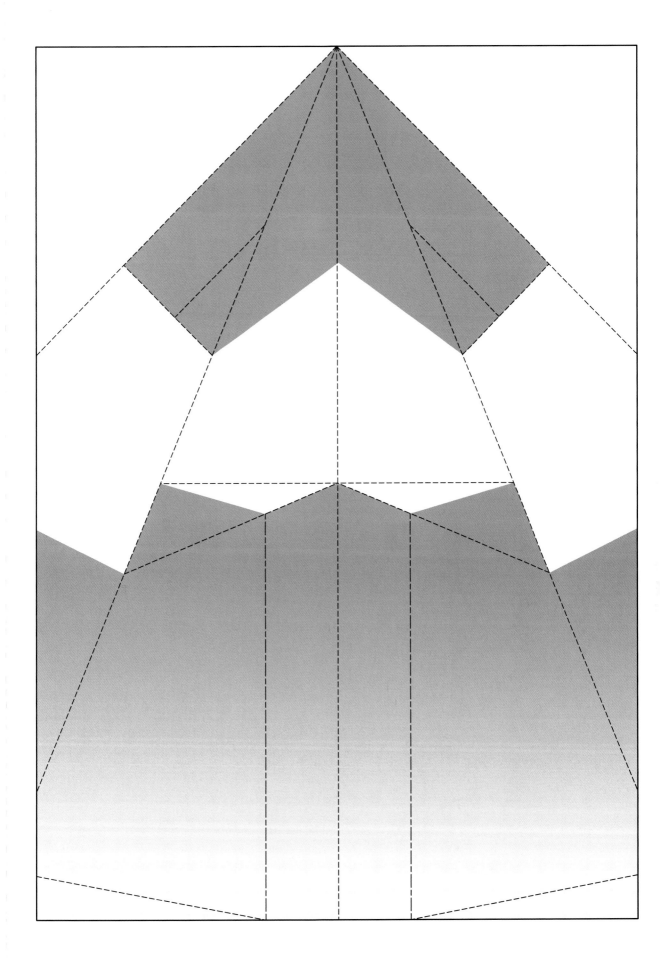

Stellar Probe Spacecraft

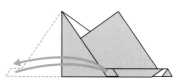

1.

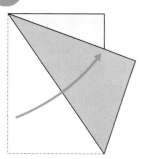

With the sheet laying printed side down, fold the sheet in half along the mountain fold line that goes from one corner to another.

2.

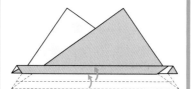

Fold up the new edge twice along the fold lines.

3.

Fold the left point across horizontally and crease along the fold line, and then unfold.

4.

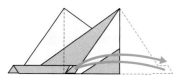

Repeat step 3 with the right side.

5.

Flip the plane over and fold in half, then unfold.

6.

Shape the plane to match the profile as shown.

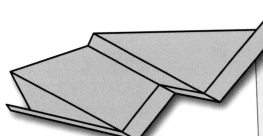

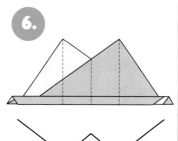

Take-off Tip
Crease the plane well and launch gently. You may need to twist the outer leading edges to achieve a smooth flight.

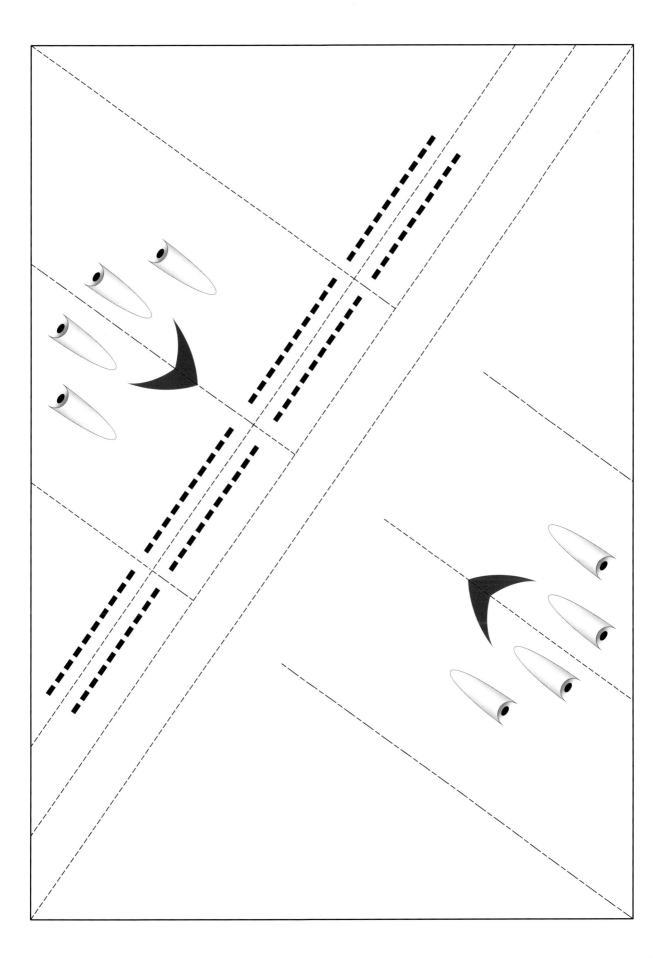

Jester Stunt Fighter

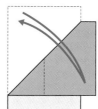

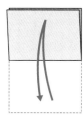

1. With the printed side up, fold in half and unfold.

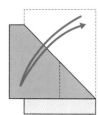

2. Flip over so printed side faces down and fold down the top right corner to bottom left along the mountain fold line and unfold.

3. Repeat with the left top corner down the the bottom right and unfold.

4. Push in the sides along the first fold and collapse to make the top a triangular shape.

5. With the blue and red striped side facing you, fold down the top point and crease along the printed mountain fold line, and unfold.

6. Take the bottom left front corner and fold up to shape as shown in the diagram, using the crease formed in step 5. Repeat with the right side.

7. Fold up the bottom edge along the fold line.

8. Flip over the plane and fold down the triangular flap.

9. Mountain fold in half.

10. Fold down the wings along the mountain fold lines. Use a small piece of sticky tape across the head to keep the two sides of the body together.

Take-off Tip

If necessary, curve the rear edges of the wings and tail between thumb and finger to achieve a smooth glide. Launch gently.

ROULETTE AEROBATIC JET

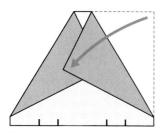

1. Make the four small cuts for the elevators. With the printed side facing up, fold the left edge to the right one along the mountain fold line, crease and then unfold.

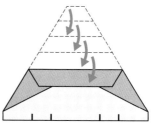

2. Flip over and diagonally fold down the top left corner along the mountain fold line.

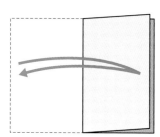

3. Repeat step 2 with the right side.

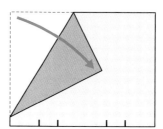

4. Fold down the top edge 4 times and crease well.

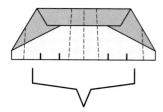

5. Fold the the plane in half, fold down the wings and fold up the wing tips to match the profile shown.

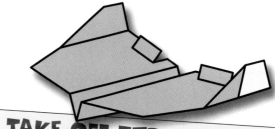

TAKE-OFF TIP
Fold up the rear elevators to about 45° to achieve a smooth glide. Launch gently.

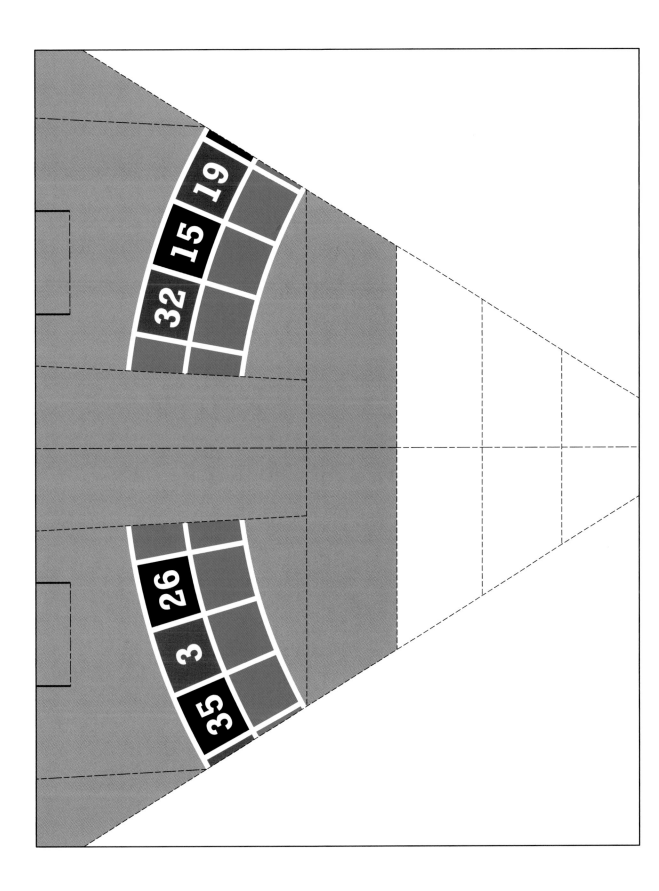

Autumn Drop Glider

1.

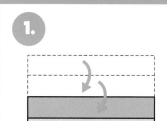

Cut the 'V' shape that will later form the tail fin. With the printed side face down, fold down the top edge twice along the mountain fold lines.

2.

Diagonally fold down the top left corner along the mountain fold line and repeat with the right side.

3.

Fold down the top point along the mountain fold line.

4.

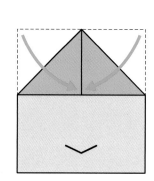

Fold up the point along the fold lines.

5.

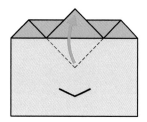

Fold the plane in half.

6.

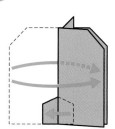

Fold the wings down and push up the tail fin.

Take-off Tip
If necessary, curve up the rear edges of the wings between thumb and finger to achieve a smooth glide. Launch gently.

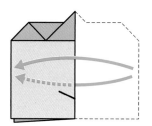

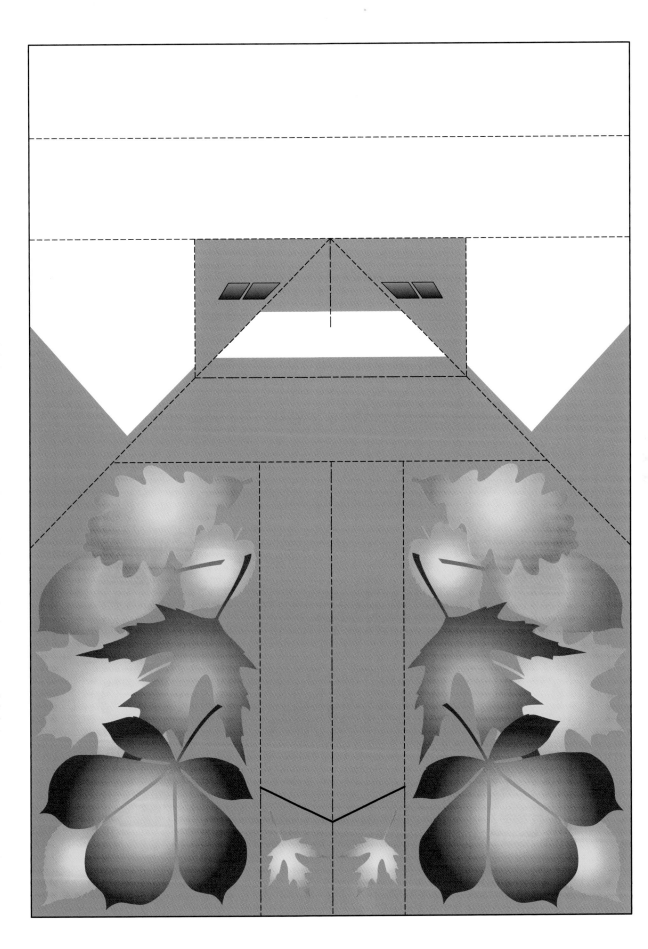

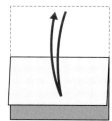

1. Cut out the main part of the plane and lay printed side face up. Fold down the top edge along the valley fold line, and then unfold.

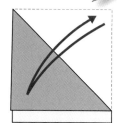

2. Flip the plane over and diagonally fold down the top right corner along the mountain fold line.

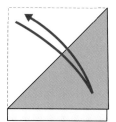

3. Repeat step 2 with the left top corner.

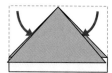

4. Push in the sides along the first fold and collapse to make the top a triangular shape.

5. Take the left loose corner of the triangle and fold diagonally up to the top. Repeat with the right side.

6. Cut out the tail and fold down the two top corners.

7. Push the tail into the plane so the point fits into the nose.

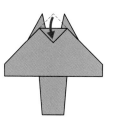

8. Fold the nose over and crease well.

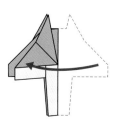

9. Fold the plane in half.

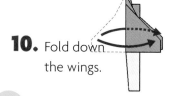

10. Fold down the wings.

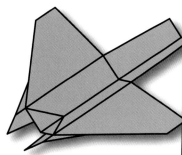

Take-off Tip

If necessary, curve up the rear edges of the tail between thumb and finger to fly in a loop. Launch forcefully.

GLOBETROTTER AIRLINER

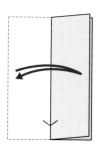

1. Cut the 'V' shape that will later form the tail fin. With the printed side facing up, fold the left edge to the right one, crease and unfold.

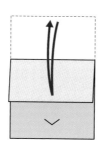

2. Fold down the top edge along the valley fold line, crease and then unfold.

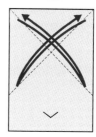

3. Flip over and diagonally fold down, crease and then unfold the top left and right corners along the mountain fold lines.

4. Push in the sides along the first fold and collapse to make the top a triangular shape.

5. Take the left loose corner of the triangle and fold diagonally up to the top, crease and then unfold. Repeat with the right side.

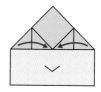

6. Fold the left point to the centre. Repeat with the right side.

7. Fold down the top point and crease along the fold line. Now take the points created in step 6 and tuck them into the pockets in the sides of the folded down point.

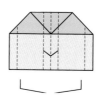

8. Fold the plane in half, fold down the wings and fold up the wing tips. Push up the tail.

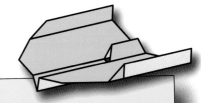

TAKE-OFF TIP
Curve up the rear edges of the wings between thumb and finger to achieve a smooth glide. Launch gently.

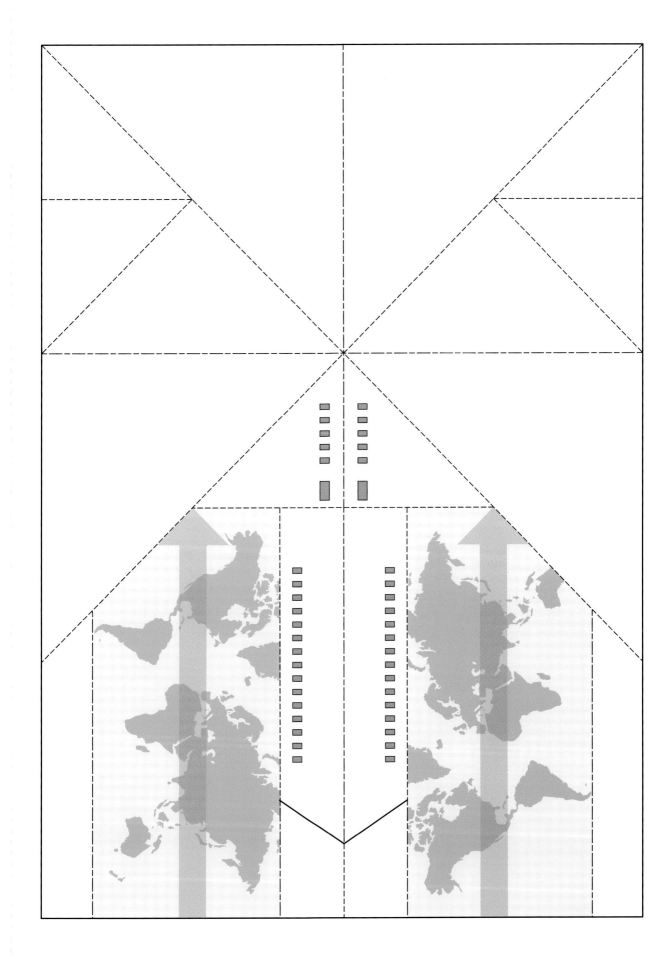

Cheetah Racing Plane

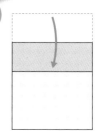

1.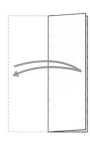

With the printed side facing up, fold the left edge to the right one, crease and then unfold.

2.

Fold the top edge down to the bottom one, crease and then unfold.

3.

Flip over so printed side faces down and fold the top edge down to the centre crease.

4.

Diagonally fold in the two top corners along the mountain fold lines.

5.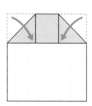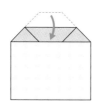

Fold the top edge down along the mountain fold line.

6.

Fold the plane in half.

7.

Diagonally fold down the top corner and unfold. Repeat the fold the other way and unfold.

8.

Take the front top edge, pull down and crease to shape.

9.

Take the rear top edge, fold behind and crease to shape.

10.

Fold down the wings.

> ### *Take-off Tip*
> **If necessary, curve up the rear edges of the wings between thumb and finger to achieve a smooth glide. Launch gently.**

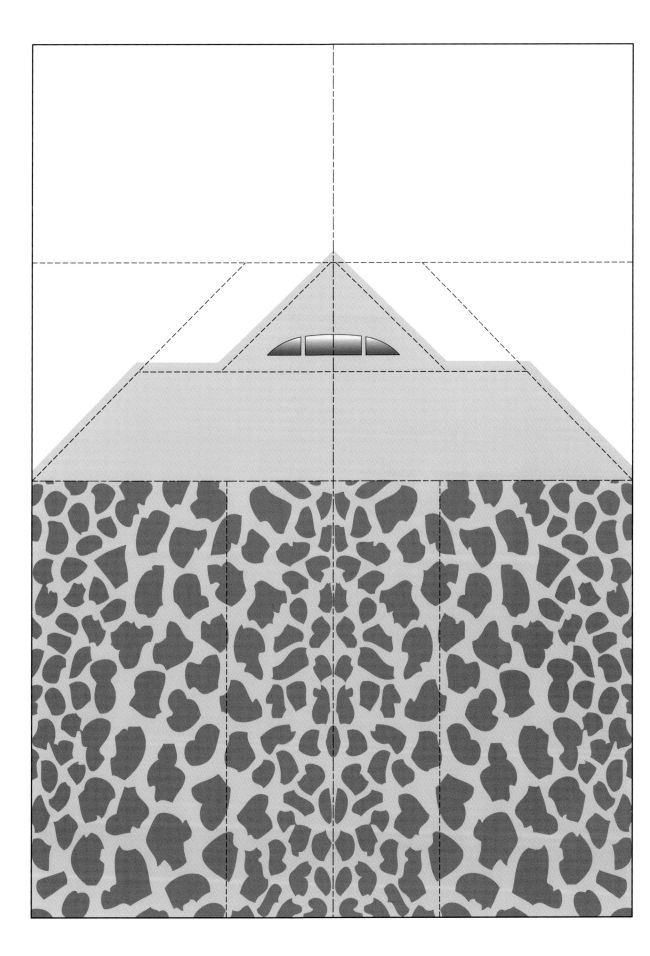

Mistral Missle

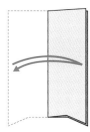

1. With the printed side facing up, fold the left edge to the right one, crease and unfold.

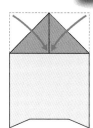

2. Diagonally fold down the top left and right corners along the mountain fold lines.

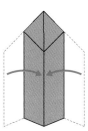

3. Fold the left and right edges into the centre crease.

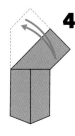

4. Diagonally fold down top left edge along the fold line, crease and unfold.

5. Repeat step 4 with the top right edge, crease and unfold.

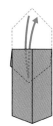

6. Fold back the top point along the mountain fold line, crease and unfold.

7. Fold the left and right edges into the centre and collapse down the top point to the same place.

8. Unfold step 7 and crease along the horizontal mountain fold line. Refold and tuck the new flap into the pocket created in step 7.

9. Diagonally fold out and crease the two bottom inner points along the valley fold lines.

Take-off Tip
Curve up the rear edges of the wings between thumb and finger to achieve a smooth glide. Launch gently.

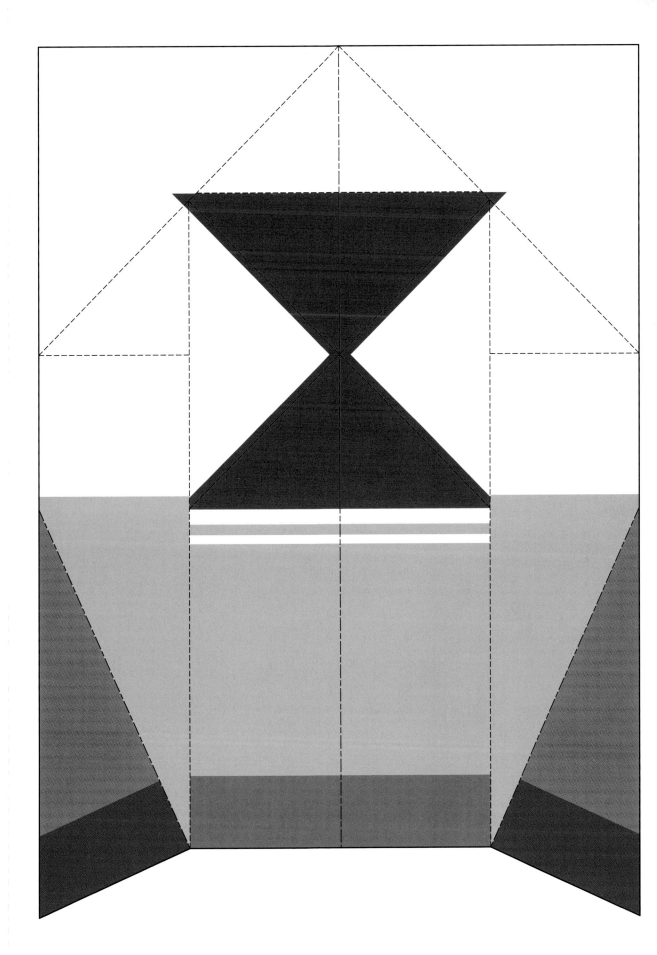

PANTHER MISSLE

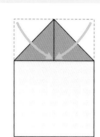
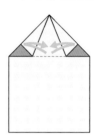

1. With the printed side facing up, fold the left edge to the right one, crease and then unfold.

2. Flip over so printed side faces down and diagonally fold in the two top corners along the mountain fold lines.

3. Fold up the two corners along the valley fold lines and then unfold.

4. Flip the plane back and fold down the top point along the valley fold line.

5. Diagonally fold up the point to the top edge along the mountain fold line and then unfold.

6. Repeat step 5 along the other valley fold line and then unfold.

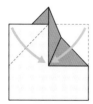
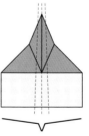

7. Fold up the point and crease along the mountain fold line.

8. Flip the plane over. Fold the left corner diagonally inwards and the plane will fall into the shape shown on the right of the diagram. Repeat with the right corner.

9. Fold the plane in half and then fold down the wings to create the profile shown.

TAKE-OFF TIP
If necessary, curve up the rear edges of the wings between thumb and finger to achieve a smooth glide. Launch gently.

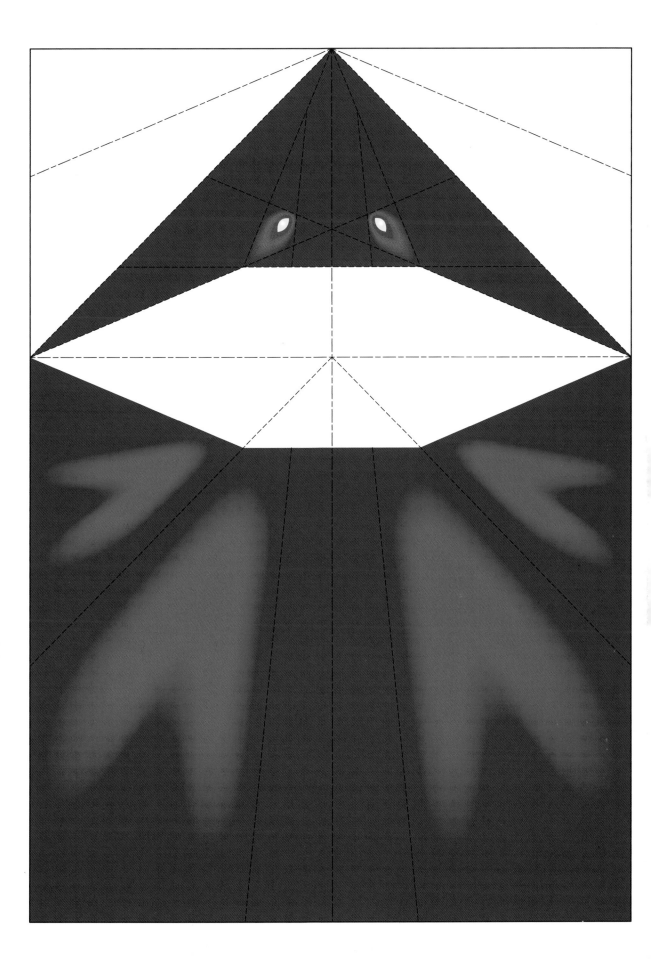

Mantis Flyer

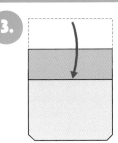

1.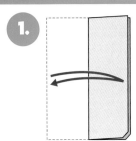

With the printed side face up, fold in half and then unfold.

2.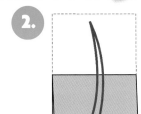

Flip over so printed side faces down and fold down the top edge to the bottom edge and unfold.

3.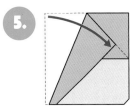

Fold down the top edge to the crease created in step 2.

4.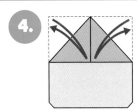

Diagonally fold the top left corner down to the centre and then unfold. Repeat with the top right corner.

5.

Fold down the top left edge to line up with the diagonal crease created on the right in step 4.

6.

Horizontally fold the point across to the left. Repeat steps 5 and 6 with the top right point.

7.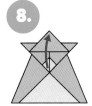

Fold down the top point along the mountain fold line.

8.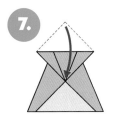

Fold up the point along the mountain fold line.

9.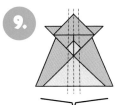

Fold in half and then fold down the wings to match the profile in the diagram.

10.

Fold in the two points horizontally along the fold lines.

Take-off Tip

If necessary, curve up the rear edges of the wings between thumb and finger to achieve a smooth glide. Launch gently.

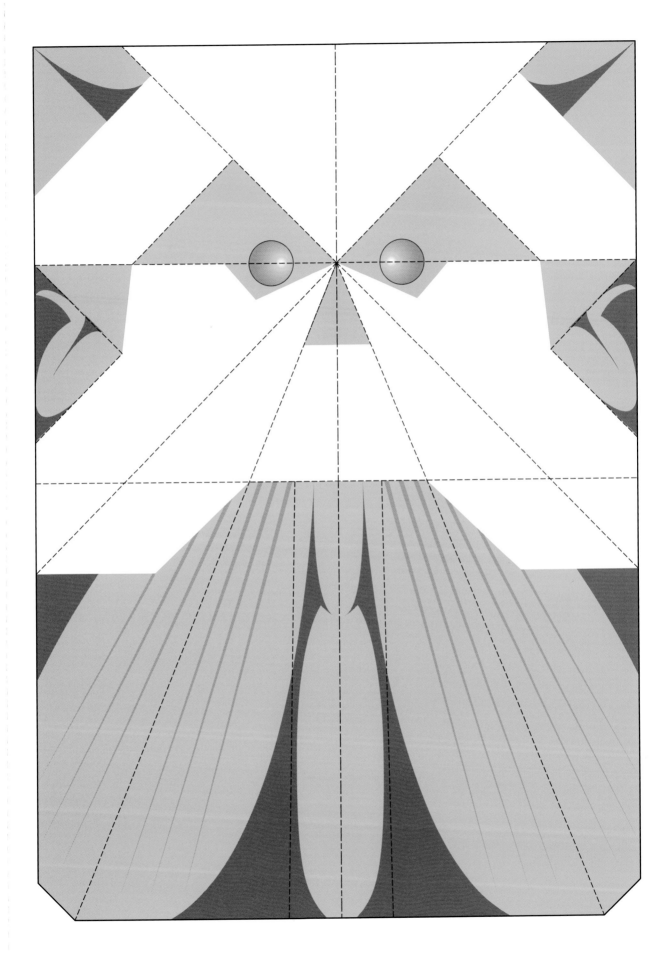

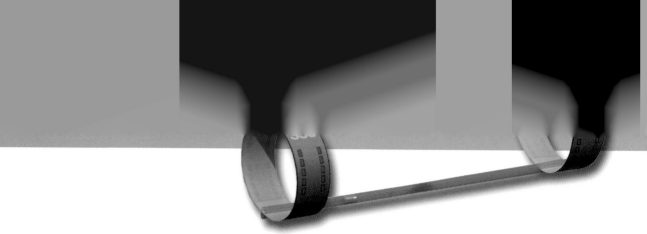

1. Cut out a long and short strip of the same colour.

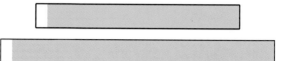

2. Make each strip into a loop by overlapping the ends and using sticky tape.

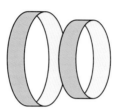

3. Take a drinking straw, pinch one end together and cut a slot long enough to take the width of a loop. Do the same at the other end making sure the cuts are at the same angle.

4. Slide the loops into the slots and stick into place with sticky tape.

Take-off Tip
To fly the plane, hold the straw with the smaller loop to the front and launch gently.

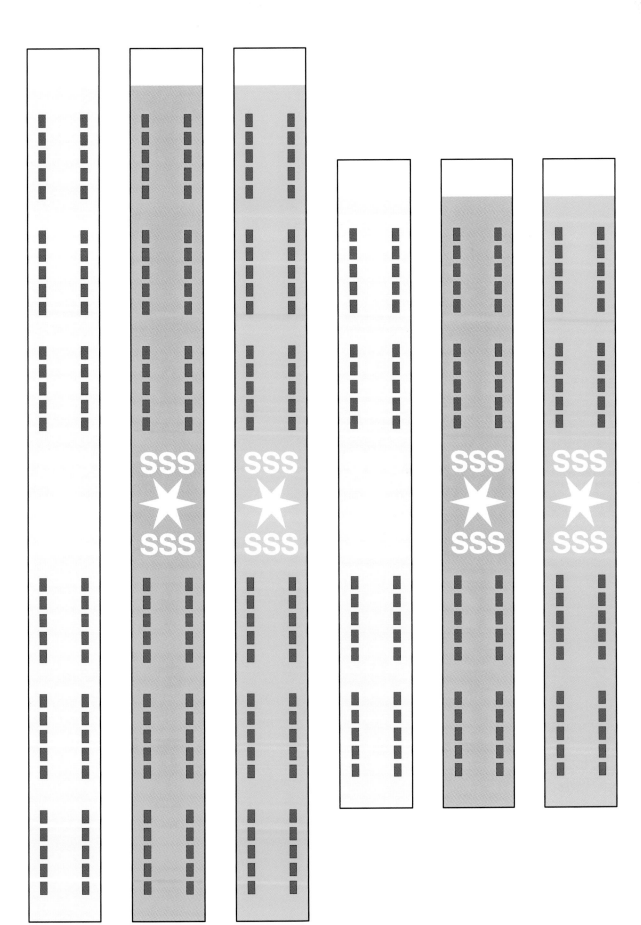

SNOWBIRD JET

1. With the printed side facing up, fold the left edge to the right one, crease and then unfold.

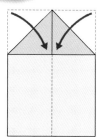

2. Fold in the two top corners along the mountain fold lines.

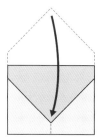

3. Fold down the top point along the mountain fold line.

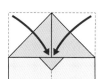

4. Fold in the two top corners along the mountain fold lines.

5. Fold up the small pointed tab along the fold line.

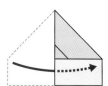

6. Fold the plane in half.

7. Fold down the wings.

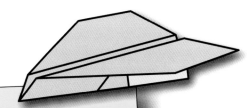

TAKE-OFF TIP
If necessary, curve up the rear edges of the wings between thumb and finger to achieve a smooth glide. Launch gently.

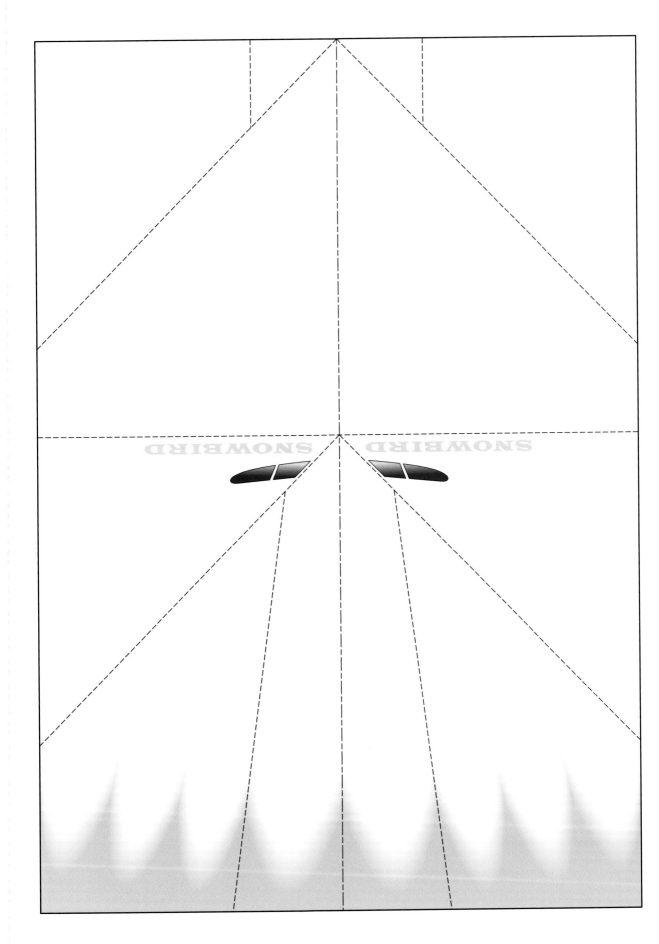

Squid Helicopter

 1.

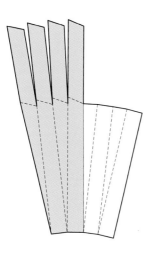

Cut out the helicopter from the sheet.

 2.

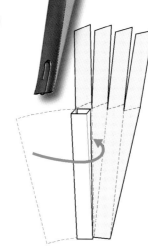

With printed side of the helicopter facing down, fold the white tabs so that the top forms a square section.

 3.

Continue folding and stick the last edge in place with a piece of sticky tape.

 4.

Fold down the four wings. Push on a paper clip and the helicopter is ready to launch by throwing up into the air.

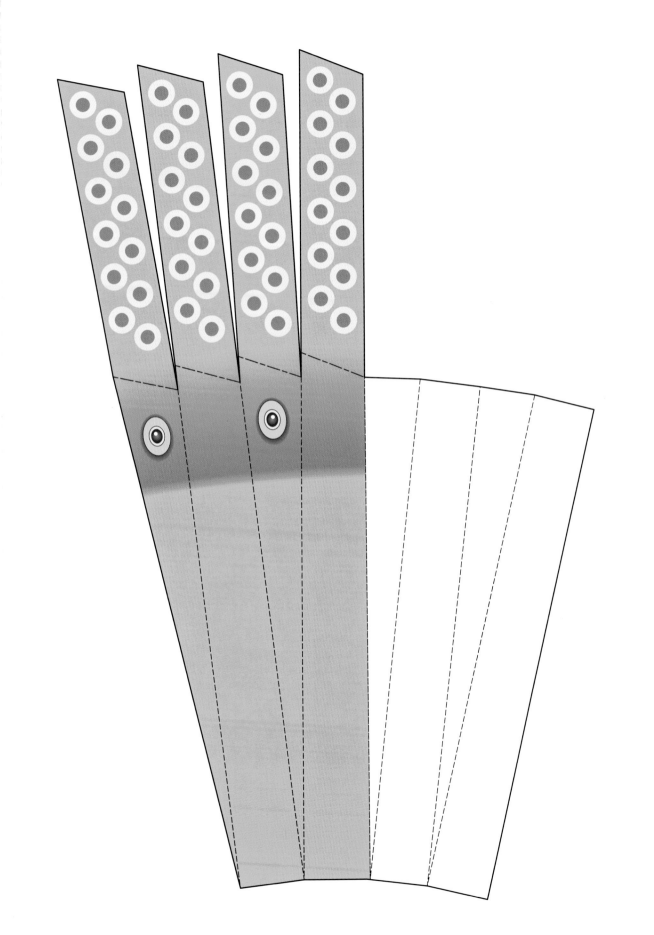

Eagle Glider

1. Lay the sheet printed side down and fold down the top edge five times.

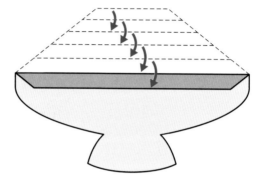

2. Fold in half, fold down the wings and fold up the wing tips to create the profile shown.

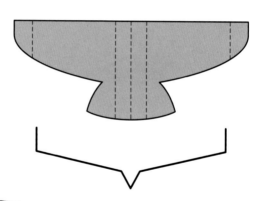

Take-off Tip
If necessary, curve up the rear edges of the wings and tail between thumb and finger to achieve a smooth glide. Launch gently.

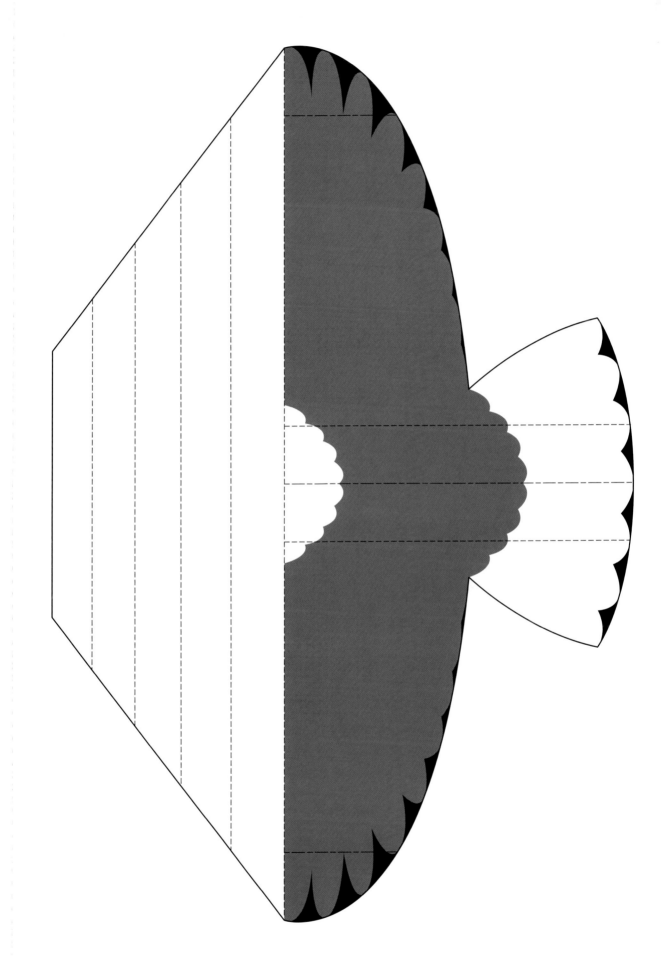

EL NINO FIGHTER

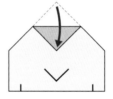

1. Cut the 'V' shape that will later form the tail and the two small cuts for the elevators. With the printed side face down fold down, the left edge across to the right edge, crease and then unfold.

2. Flip the plane over and diagonally fold down the top left corner along the mountain fold line and repeat with the right side.

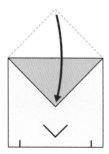

3. Fold down the top triangle along the mountain fold line.

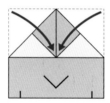

4. Flip the plane over and diagonally fold down the two top corners.

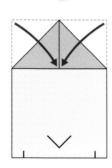

5. Flip the plane back and fold down the top point.

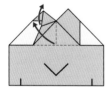

6. Flip the plane over again and crease the small diagonal folds and then lift the folds upwards and crease the new shape.

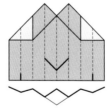

7. Fold the mountain and valley folds to create the profile shown.

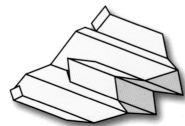

TAKE-OFF TIP
Fold up the rear elevators to achieve a smooth glide. Launch gently.

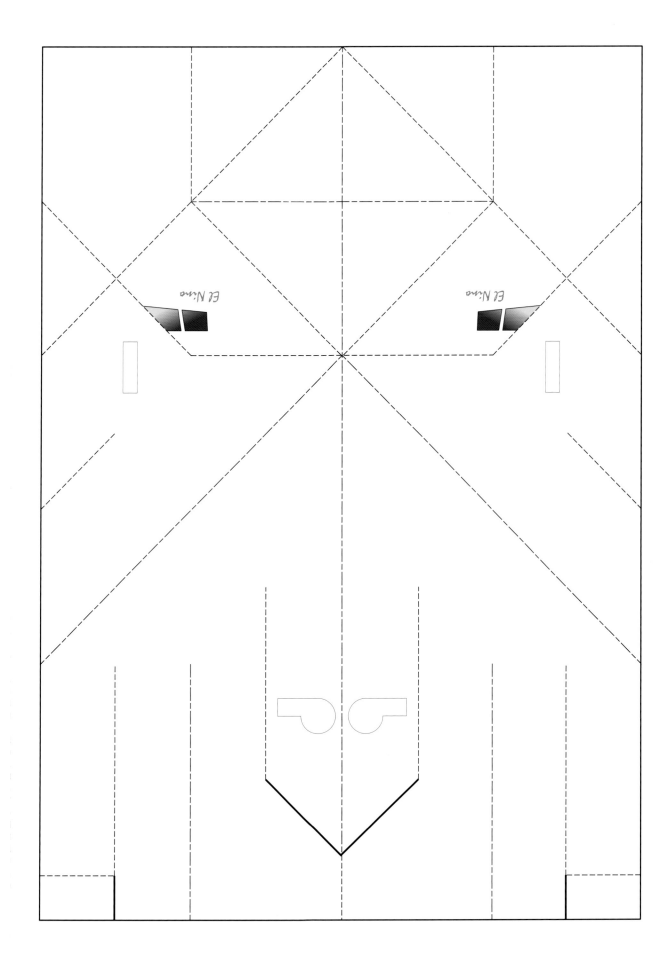

Devastation Bomber

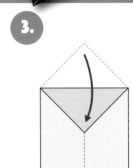

1.

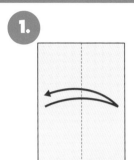

With the printed side face down, fold in half and then unfold.

2.

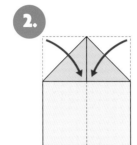

Fold the top left corner into the central crease. Repeat with the right corner.

3.

Fold the top point downwards.

4.

Fold the point upwards to the printed line.

5.

Fold the top left corner into the centre then crease and unfold. Repeat with right corner.

6.

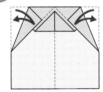

Fold the left edge to the crease created in 5 and then unfold. Repeat with the right edge.

7.

Fold the large right angled triangles created in 5 over again. Tuck the flaps created in 6 under the tip folded in 4.

8.

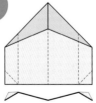

Valley fold the central crease and mountain fold the two lines on the wings. Fold up the two small elevators to about 45°.

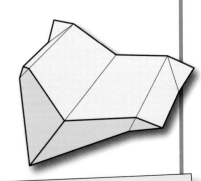

Take-off Tip

When launching, don't throw the plane. Just release it while moving your hand slowly forward. Adjust the elevators to achieve a smooth glide.

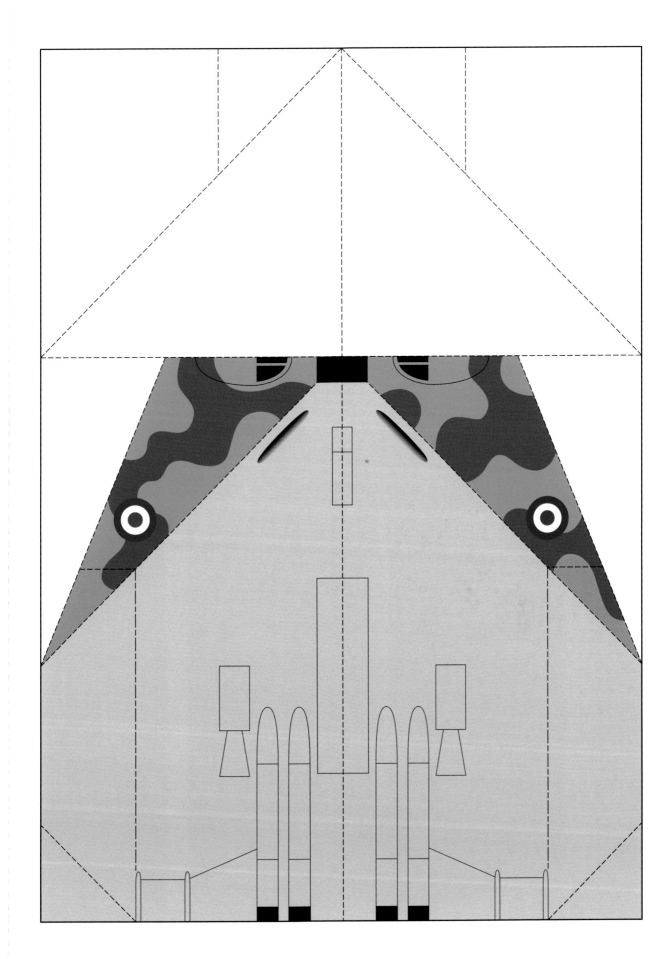

Seastride Airliner

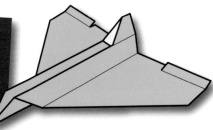

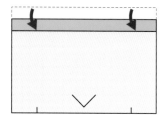

1. Cut the 'V' shape that will later form the tail fin and the two small cuts for the elevators. With the printed side face down, fold down the long top edge along the mountain fold line.

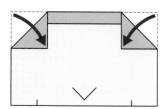

2. Diagonally fold down the top left corner along the mountain fold line and repeat with the right side.

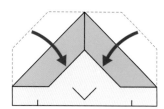

3. Fold the new top edges diagonally along the mountain fold lines.

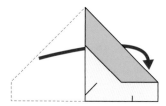

4. Fold the plane in half.

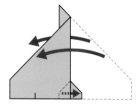

5. Fold the sides down and push up the tail fin.

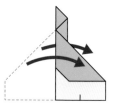

6. Fold up the wings.

Take-off Tip
Fold up the rear elevators to achieve a smooth glide. Launch gently.

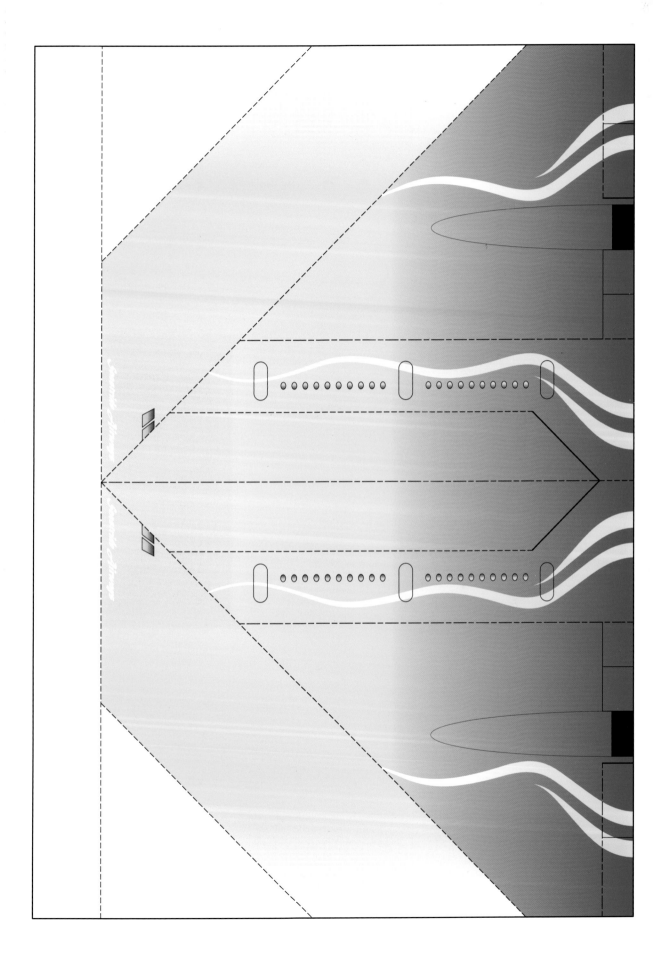

BLUE STREAK RACING PLANE

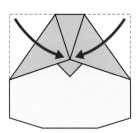

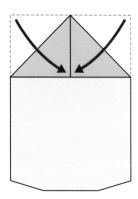

1. Lay the sheet printed side down and diagonally fold in the two top corners.

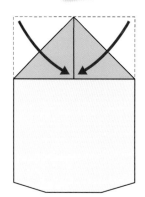

2. Fold down the top point along the mountain fold line.

3. Fold the two new top corners into the centre along the mountain fold lines.

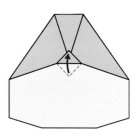

4. Fold up the small tab.

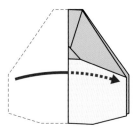

5. Fold the plane in half.

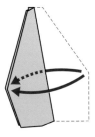

6. Fold down the wings.

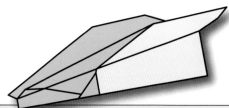

TAKE-OFF TIP
If necessary, curve up the rear edges of the wings between thumb and finger to achieve a smooth glide. Launch at a moderate speed.

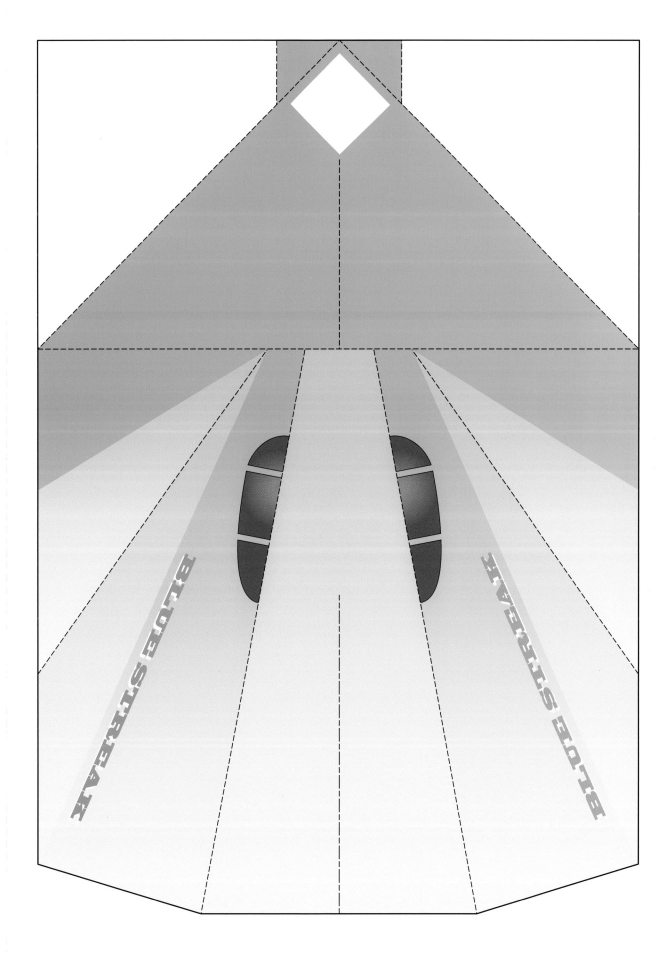

Thor Fighter

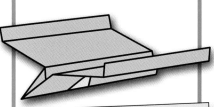

1.

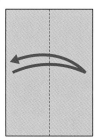

With the printed side face up, fold in half and then unfold.

2.

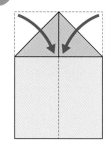

Flip over so printed side faces down and diagonally fold in the two top corners to the centre.

3.

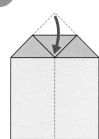

Fold down the top tip along the mountain fold line.

4.

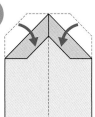

Fold down the two new top edges along the mountain fold lines.

5.

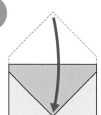

Fold down the top tip to line up with the bottom edge.

6.

Fold up the tip and crease along the mountain fold line.

7.

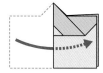

Fold the plane in half.

8.

Fold down the wings and fold up the wing tips

Take-off Tip

If necessary, curve up the rear edges of the wings between thumb and finger to achieve a smooth glide. Launch gently.

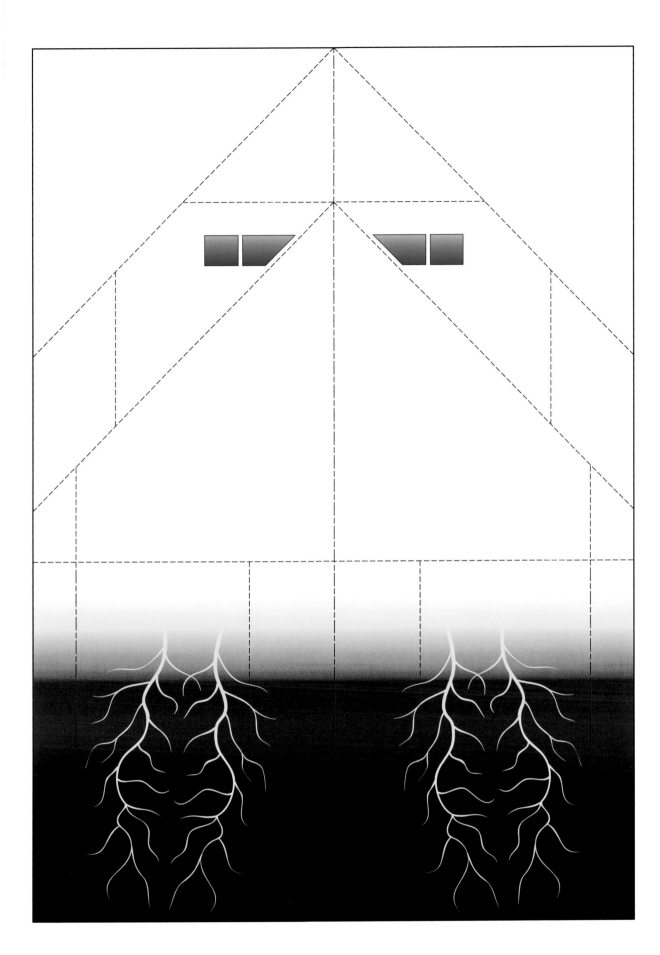

Mosquito Stunt Flyer

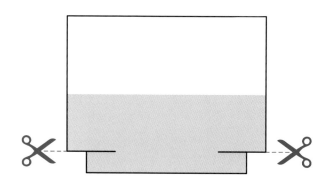

1. Cut the two slots that will later form the tail fins.

2. Flip over so printed side faces down and fold down the top edge five times. Crease well.

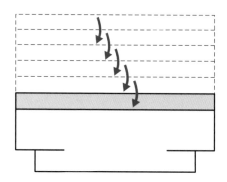

3. Fold the plane in half. Open up to form a dihedral and fold up the two tail fins.

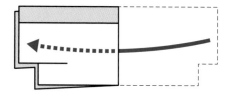

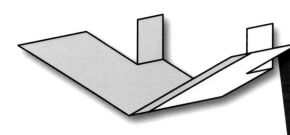

Take-off Tip

Launch gently. Adjust the elevators to achieve a smooth glide.

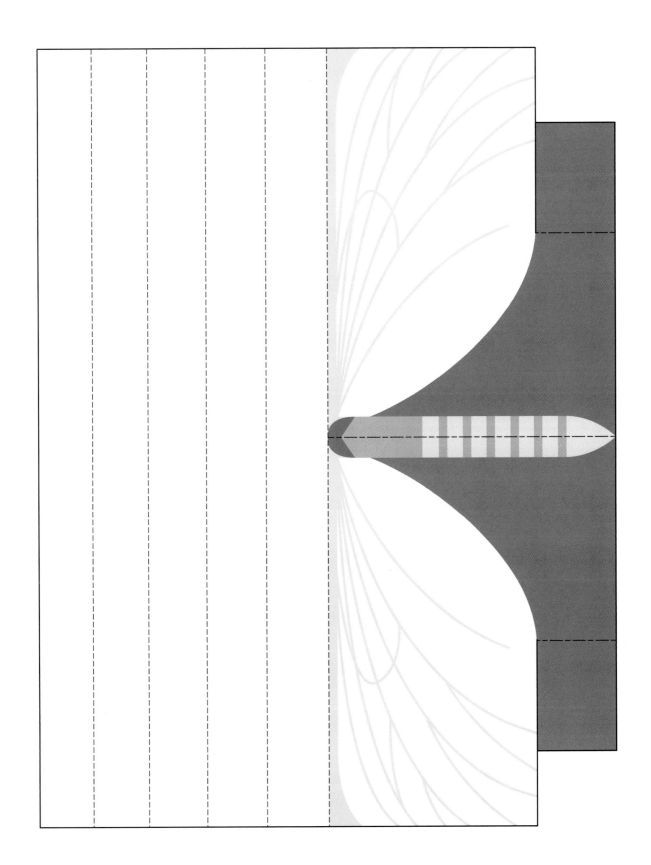

LUNAR EXPRESS SPACECRAFT

1. With the printed side face down fold in the top two corners to the centre.

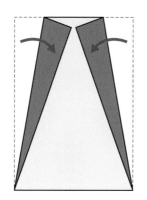

2. Fold down six times.

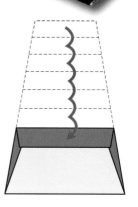

3. Flip over so printed side faces up and fold in half.

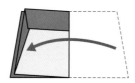

4. Fold down the wings.

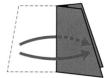

5. Fold up the two wing tips.

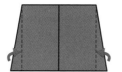

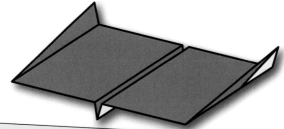

TAKE-OFF TIP
If necessary, curve up the rear edges of the wings between thumb and finger to achieve a smooth glide. Launch gently.

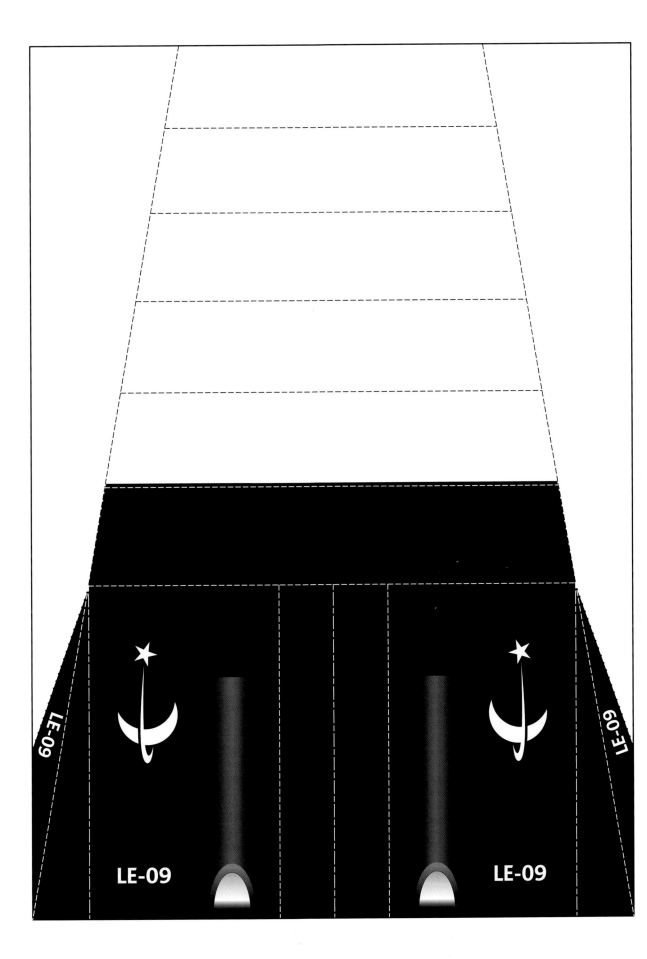

Harlequin Racing Plance

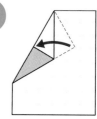

1.

With the printed side facing up, fold the left edge to the right one, crease and then unfold.

2.

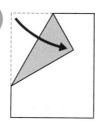

Flip over so printed side faces down and diagonally fold in the top left corner along the mountain fold line.

3.

Horizontally fold the point back to the left edge along the valley fold line.

4.

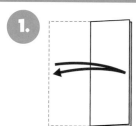

Repeat steps 2 and 3 with the top right corner. Your plane should now look like this.

5.

Flip over and fold down the top point along the mountain fold line.

6.

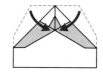

Flip the plan back over again and diagonally fold the two top corners down to the centre along the mountain fold lines.

7.

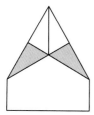

Flip the plane over and fold up the point, crease and then unfold.

8.

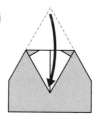

Lift up the two centre pockets folding along the crease created in step 7 and collapse and crease to make the shape shown in step 9.

9.

Fold the plane in half and then fold down the wings.

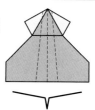

Take-off Tip
If necessary, curve up the rear edges of the wings between thumb and finger to achieve a smooth glide. Launch gently.

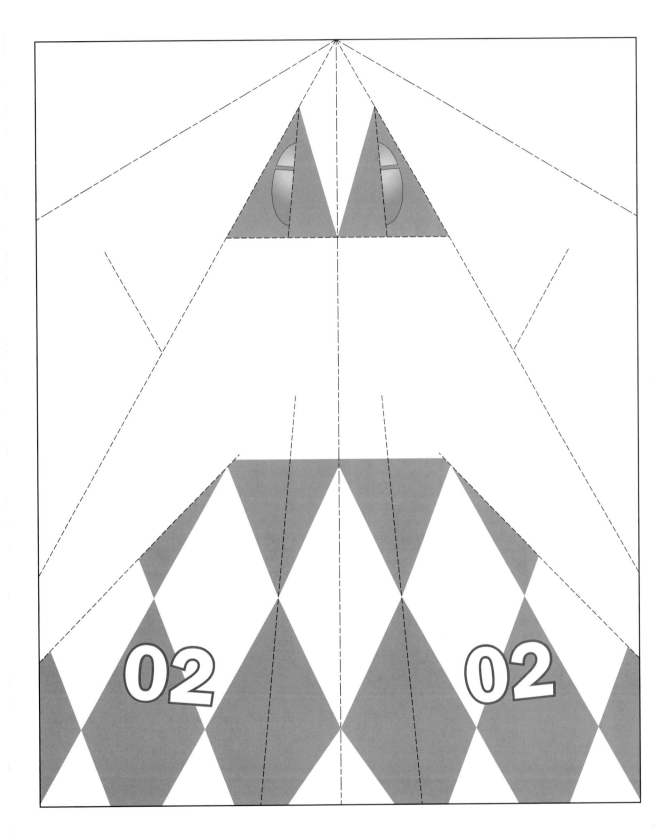

Airblade Glider

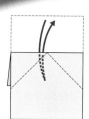

1. With the printed side face down, diagonally fold down the top left corner along the mountain fold line, crease and then unfold. Repeat with the right corner.

2. Fold the top edge back along the valley fold line and then unfold.

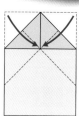

3. Fold the two top corners diagonally into the centre.

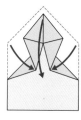

4. Fold the left and right points into the centre and fold down the top point to the same place.

5. Fold back the tip along the longer of the two mountain fold lines. Fold up the two small flaps and then unfold.

6. Pull up the central point and fold the small flaps into shape as shown.

7. Flip over the plane and fold up the small flap, the fold down the smaller flap.

8. Fold the plane in half.

9. Fold down the wings. Use a small piece of sticky tape to hold the top of the 'cockpit' together.

Take-off Tip
Fold up the rear elevators to achieve a smooth glide. Launch gently.

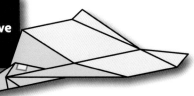

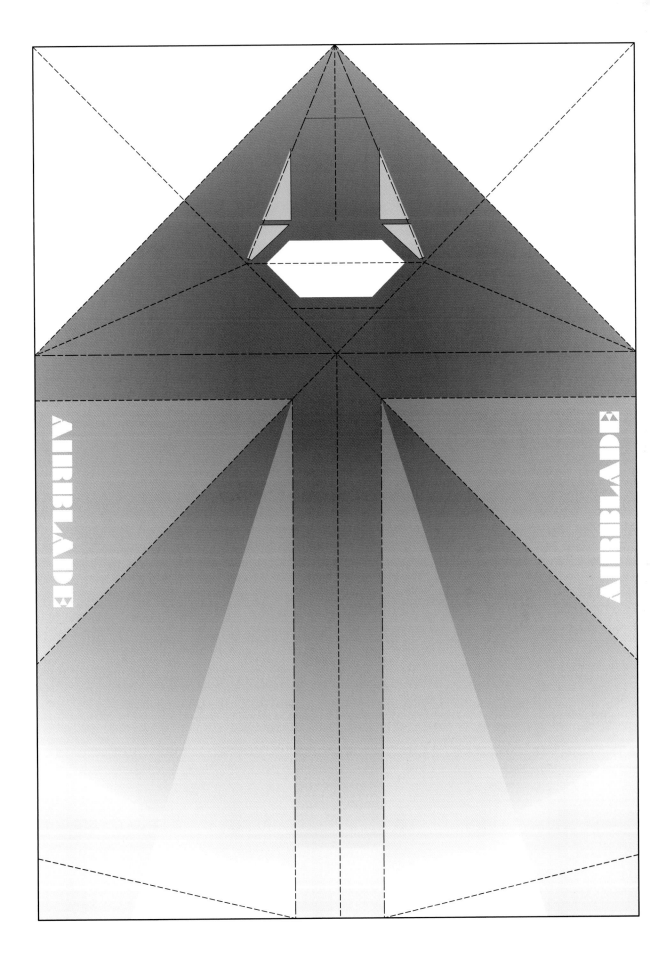

THUNDERCLAP BOMBER

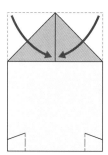

1. Make the small cuts for the tail fins. With the printed side face down fold in the top two corners to the centre.

2. Fold down the top point along the mountain fold line.

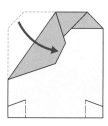

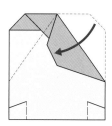

3. Diagonally fold down the top left edge and crease along the mountain fold line.

4. Fold back the flap created in step 3 and repeat with the right side.

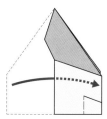

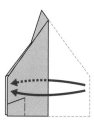

5. Fold again the left side and fold the plane in half.

6. Fold down the wings and fold up the tail fins.

TAKE-OFF TIP
If necessary, curve up the rear edges of the wings between thumb and finger to achieve a smooth glide. Launch gently.

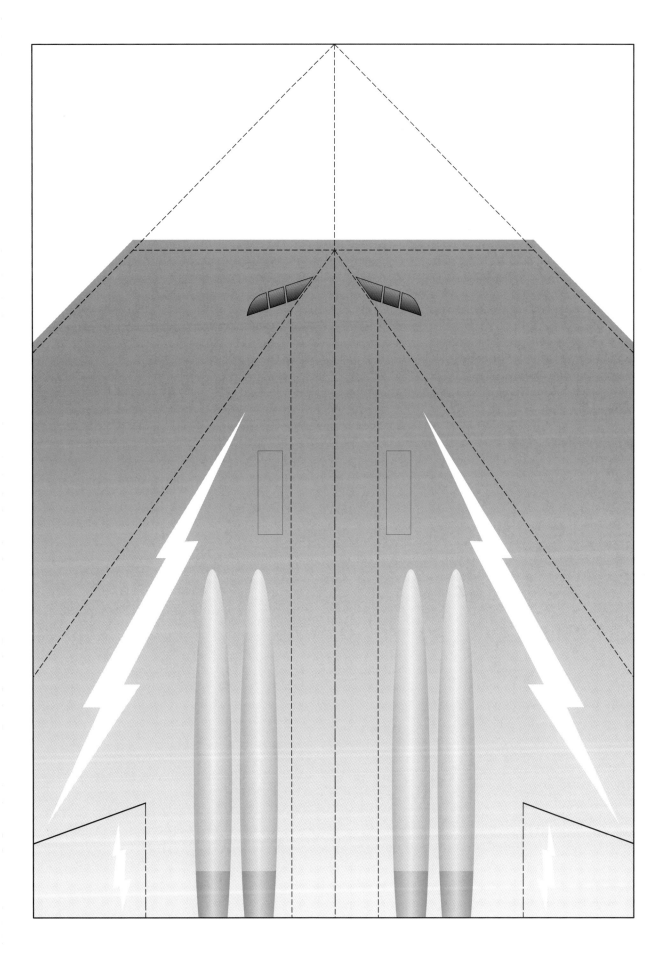

Bat Glider

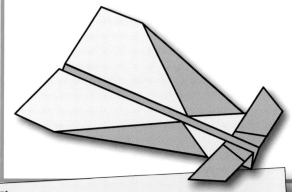

1. 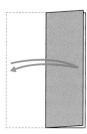 With the printed side facing down, fold the left edge to the right one, crease and unfold.

2. 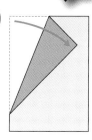 Diagonally fold down the top left corner along the mountain fold line.

3.  Valley fold the point to the left along the fold line.

4.  Repeat steps 2 and 3 with the right side of the plane. Your plane should now look like this.

5. 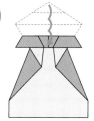 Fold down the top point three times along the fold lines.

6. Fold the model in half.

7. Fold down both wings. Stick the front edges of the fuselage together with a small piece of sticky tape.

Take-off Tip
If necessary, curve up the rear edges of the wings between thumb and finger to achieve a smooth glide. Launch gently.

Meteor Racing Plane

1. With the printed side face up, fold in half and unfold.

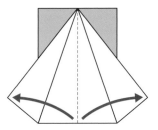

2. Flip over so printed side faces down and fold in the two outer edges to the centre.

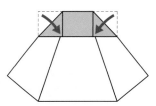

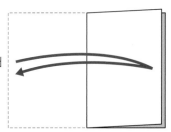

3. Fold out the bottom corners from the centre along the valley fold lines.

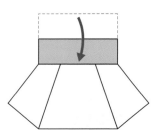

4. Fold down the top edge.

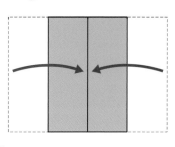

5. Diagonally fold in the two top corners.

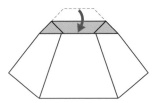

6. Fold down the top edge along the mountain fold line.

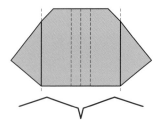

7. Fold in half, fold down the wings and fold down the wing ends to create the profile shown. Tape the two front edges of the body together with a small piece of sticky tape.

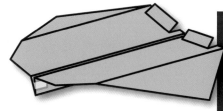

Take-off Tip
Fold up the elevators to achieve a smooth glide. Launch gently.

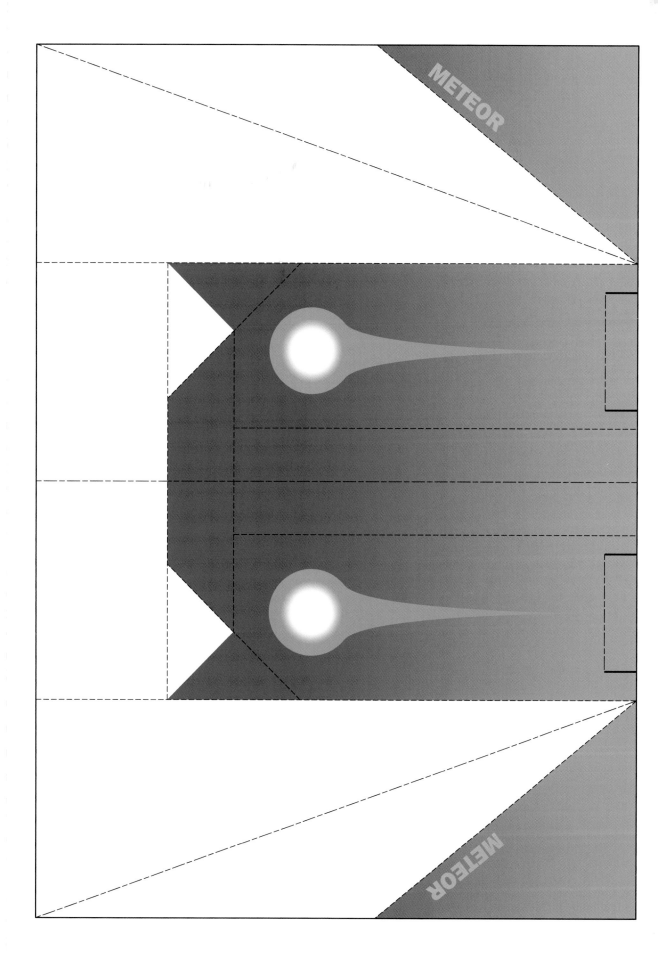

BUCCANEER FIGHTER

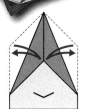

1. Cut the 'V' shape that will later form the tail fin. With the printed side up fold in half and unfold.

2. Flip over so printed side faces down and diagonally fold down the top left and right corners to to the centre fold.

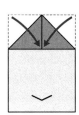

3. Fold the new side points into the centre along the mountain fold lines, crease and then unfold.

4. Fold the two points to the crease line created in step 3 along the mountain fold lines.

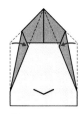

5. Fold the sides in along the creases created in step 3.

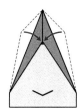

6. Flip the plane over and fold the top point down along the mountain fold line.

7. Fold the point up along the fold line.

8. Fold in half.

9. Fold down the wings along the mountain fold lines and push up the tail fin. Use a small piece of sticky tape across the front to keep the two sides of the body together.

TAKE-OFF TIP
If necessary, curve the rear edges of the wings and tail between thumb and finger to achieve a smooth glide. Launch gently.

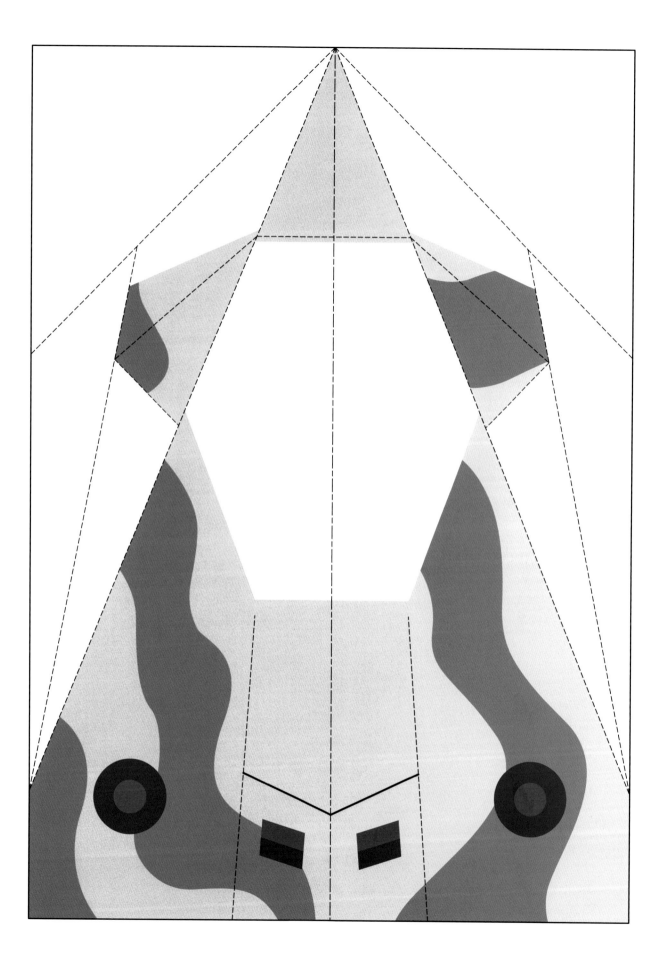

Flashdance Flyer

1.

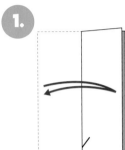

Cut the 'V' shape that will later form the tail fin. With the printed side up fold in half and unfold.

2.

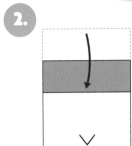

Flip over so printed side faces down and fold down the top along the mountain fold line.

3.

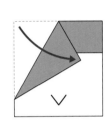

Diagonally fold the top left point along the mountain fold line.

4.

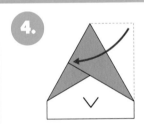

Diagonally fold the top right point along the mountain fold line.

5.

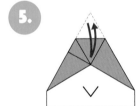

Fold down the top point along the mountain fold line, crease and then unfold.

6.

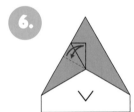

Fold the left point, created in step 4, to the centre along the fold line, crease and then unfold.

7.

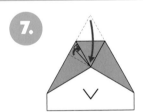

Now fold down the top point again and push the tab formed in step 6 into the pocket in its side.

8.

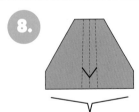

Fold the plane in half and then fold down the wings to form the profile shown. Push up the tail and crease.

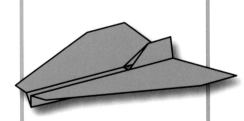

Take-off Tip
If necessary, curve the rear edges of the wings between thumb and finger to achieve a smooth glide. Launch gently.

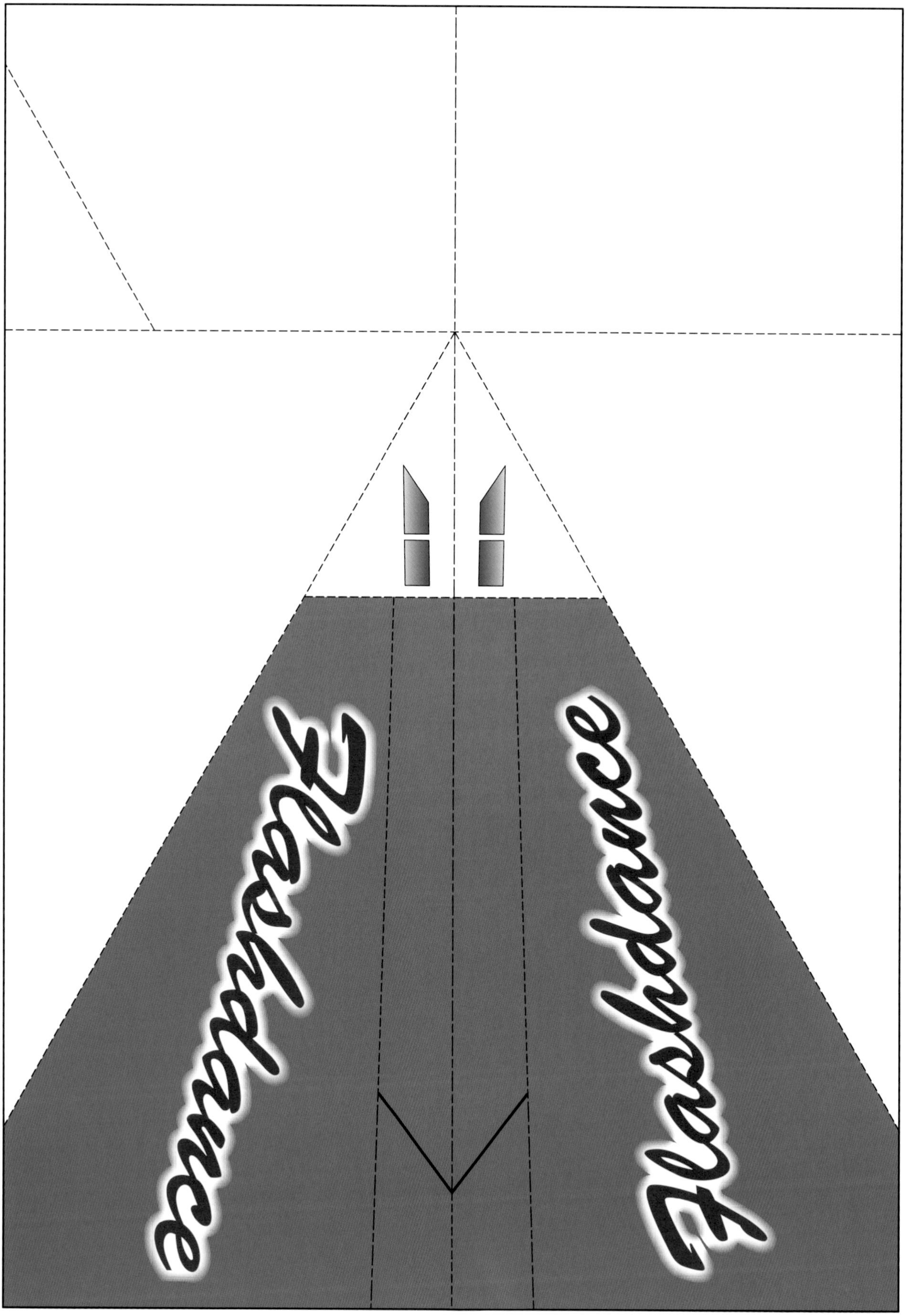
Flashdance
Flashdance

1. With the printed side face down, fold in half and then unfold.

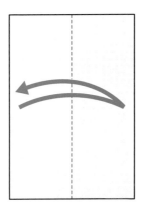

2. Fold the top left corner into the central crease. Repeat with the right corner.

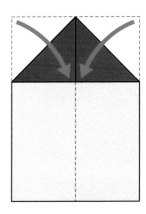

3. Fold the top left edge into the central crease. Repeat with the right edge.

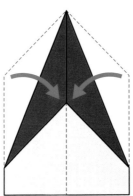

4. Valley fold the plane in half.

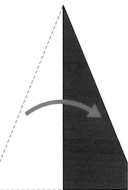

5. Fold down the wings and fold up the rear elevators slightly.

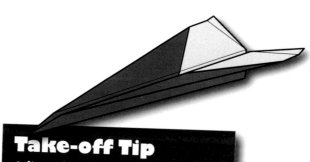

Take-off Tip
Adjust the elevators to achieve a smooth glide. Launch gently.

STEALTH SUPER JET

1. Cut the 'V' shape that will form the tail. With the printed side face down, fold in half and then unfold.

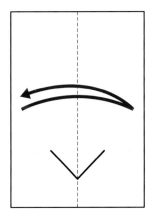

2. Fold the top left corner into the central crease. Repeat with the right corner.

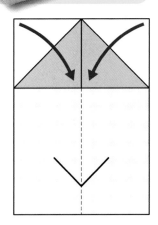

3. Fold the top left edge into the central crease. Repeat with the right edge.

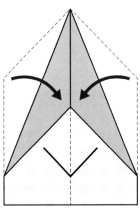

4. Fold down the top point along the mountain fold line.

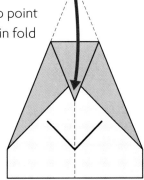

5. Fold the plane in half and then crease and fold the wings down, at the same time folding up the tip of the tail to create the profile shown.

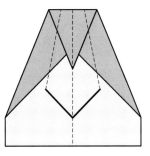

TAKE-OFF TIP
If necessary, curve the rear edges of the wings between thumb and finger to achieve a smooth glide. Launch gently.

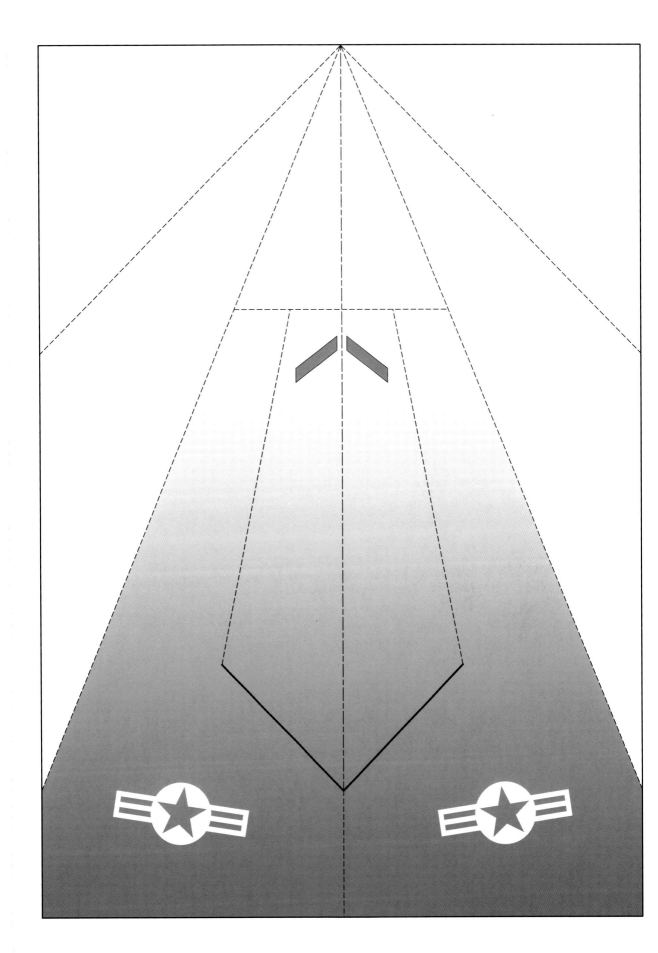

Golden Flame Racing Plane

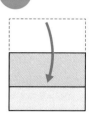

1.

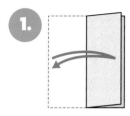

With the printed side facing up, fold the left edge to the right one, crease and then unfold.

2.

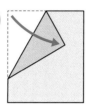

Flip over so printed side faces down and diagonally fold in the top left corner along the mountain fold line, then unfold.

3.

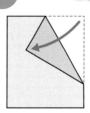

Repeat step 2 with the top right corner.

4.

Fold down the top edge along the mountain fold line.

5.

Diagonally fold the top two corners along the mountain fold lines, crease and then unfold. Fold again but this time fold back, crease and and then unfold.

6.

Take the left corner of the front fold and position along the top edge as shown and crease to the new shape.

7.

Repeat step 6 with the right corner of the front fold.

8.

Your plane should now look like this.

9.

Diagonally fold the top left point down along the mountain fold line. Repeat for top right point.

10.

Fold up the middle point and crease well.

11.

Fold the plane in half.

12.

Fold down the wings and fold down the wing tips.

Take-off Tip

If necessary, curve down the rear edges of the wings between thumb and finger to achieve a smooth glide. Launch gently.

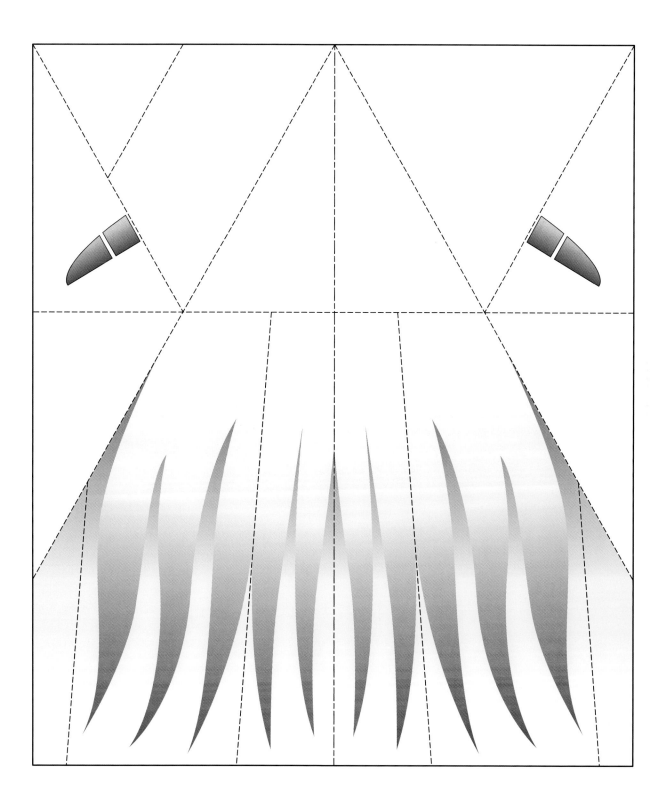

Starwing Glider

Take-off Tip

If necessary, curve up the rear edges of the wings between thumb and finger to achieve a smooth glide. Launch gently.

1. With the printed side face up, fold in half and then unfold.

2. Flip over so printed side faces down and fold down the top left corner diagonally along the mountain fold line and unfold. Repeat with the right corner and unfold.

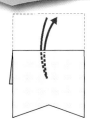

3. Fold back the top edge along the valley fold line and then unfold.

4. Push in the sides along the valley folds and collapse to make a triangular shape.

5. Take the left loose corner of the triangle and fold diagonally up to the top and then unfold. Repeat with the right side.

6. Take the same left loose corner in step 5 and fold inwards to the centre and then unfold. Repeat with the right side.

7. Fold down the top point to line up with the bottom centre of the triangle, crease and the unfold.

8. The plane with its creased lines should now look like this.

9. Lift the single bottom edge of the triangle, fold it up and crease along the valley fold line. Lift up the two bottom corners of the triangle and position them over the top point.

10. Crease and your plane should now look like this.

11. Diagonally fold out the two top inner points.

12. Fold down the top flap along the mountain fold line.

13. Fold in half.

14. Fold down the wings.

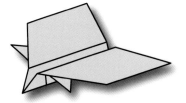

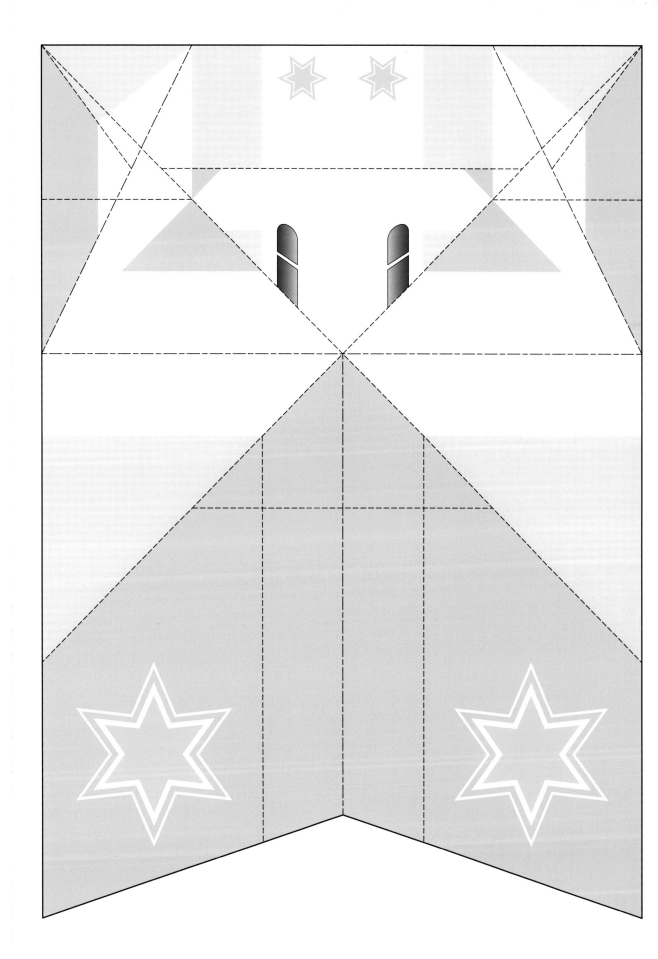

JUGGLER STUNT FLYER

1. Cut out the square that is the main part of the plane and with the printed side face down fold the bottom right corner up the top left, crease and then unfold.

2. Repeat step 1 with the bottom right corner.

3. Flip over so printed side faces up and fold the bottom edge up to the top edge, crease and then unfold.

4. Fold the left edge over to the right edge, crease and then unfold.

5. Push in the sides along the valley folds and collapse to make a triangular shape.

6. Take the left loose corner of the triangle and fold diagonally up to the top. Repeat with the right side.

7. Fold up the left corner of the new triangle and crease along the fold line and unfold. Repeat with the right side and unfold.

8. Fold down the left corner of the new triangle and crease along the fold line and unfold. Repeat with the right side and unfold.

   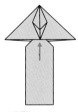

9. Crease the small folds between those just created and pinch, press down and crease the folds.

10. Fold back the two points created in step 9.

11. Cut out the tail and fold down the two top corners.

12. Push the tail into the plane so the point fits into the nose.

13. Fold the nose over.

14. Fold the plane in half.

TAKE-OFF TIP
If necessary, curve up the rear edges of the tail between thumb and finger to fly in a loop. Launch forcefully.

190

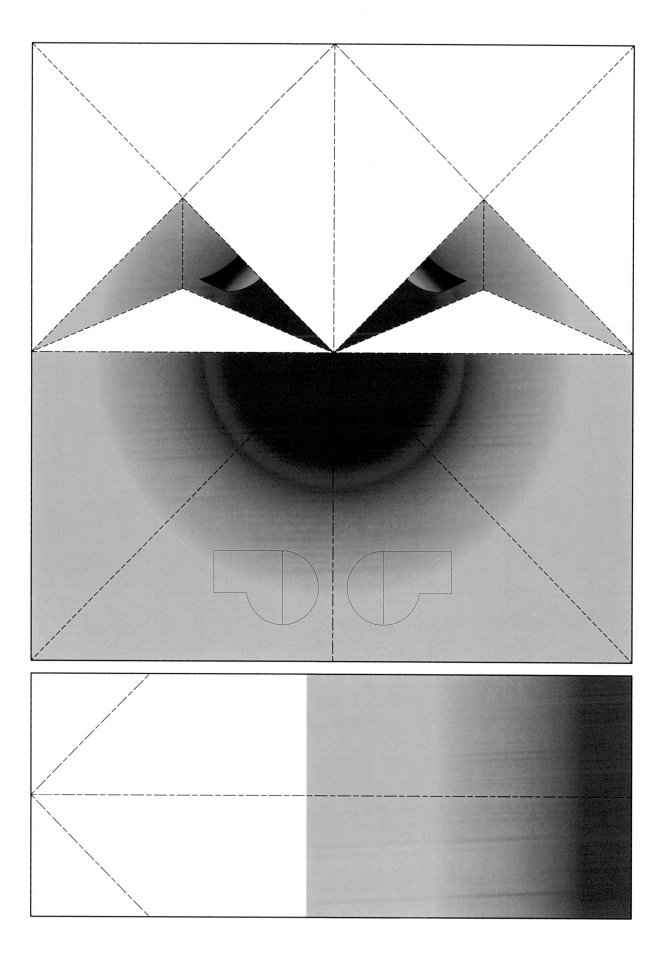